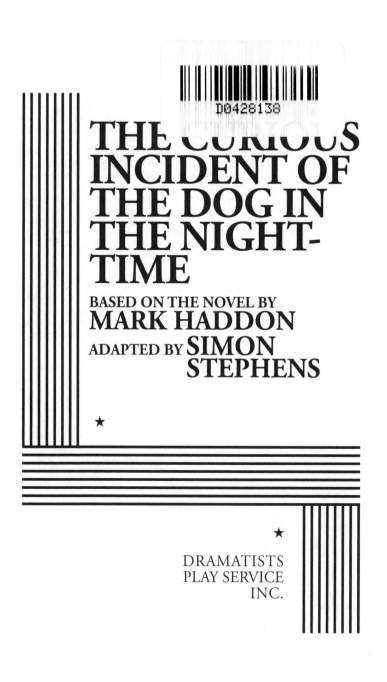

D0428138

THE CURIOUS INCIDENT OF THE DOG IN THE NIGHT-TIME

BASED ON THE NOVEL BY
MARK HADDON
ADAPTED BY **SIMON STEPHENS**

★

★

DRAMATISTS
PLAY SERVICE
INC.

THE CURIOUS INCIDENT OF THE DOG IN THE NIGHT-TIME
Copyright © 2015, Simon Stephens

All Rights Reserved

CAUTION: Professionals and amateurs are hereby warned that performance of THE CURIOUS INCIDENT OF THE DOG IN THE NIGHT-TIME is subject to payment of a royalty. It is fully protected under the copyright laws of the United States of America, and of all countries covered by the International Copyright Union (including the Dominion of Canada and the rest of the British Commonwealth), and of all countries covered by the Pan-American Copyright Convention, the Universal Copyright Convention, the Berne Convention, and of all countries with which the United States has reciprocal copyright relations. All rights, including without limitation professional/amateur stage rights, motion picture, recitation, lecturing, public reading, radio broadcasting, television, video or sound recording, all other forms of mechanical, electronic and digital reproduction, transmission and distribution, such as CD, DVD, the Internet, private and file-sharing networks, information storage and retrieval systems, photocopying, and the rights of translation into foreign languages are strictly reserved. Particular emphasis is placed upon the matter of readings, permission for which must be secured from the Author's agent in writing.

The English language stock and amateur stage performance rights in the United States, its territories, possessions and Canada for THE CURIOUS INCIDENT OF THE DOG IN THE NIGHT-TIME are controlled exclusively by DRAMATISTS PLAY SERVICE, INC., 440 Park Avenue South, New York, NY 10016. No professional or nonprofessional performance of the Play may be given without obtaining in advance the written permission of DRAMATISTS PLAY SERVICE, INC., and paying the requisite fee.

Inquiries concerning all other rights should be addressed to Casarotto Ramsay & Associates, Ltd., Waverley House, 7-12 Noel Street, London, W1F 8GQ, England. Attn: Mel Kenyon.

SPECIAL NOTE

Anyone receiving permission to produce THE CURIOUS INCIDENT OF THE DOG IN THE NIGHT-TIME is required to give credit to the Author(s) as sole and exclusive Author(s) of the Play on the title page of all programs distributed in connection with performances of the Play and in all instances in which the title of the Play appears, including printed or digital materials for advertising, publicizing or otherwise exploiting the Play and/or a production thereof. Please see your production license for font size and typeface requirements.

Be advised that there may be additional credits required in all programs and promotional material. Such language will be listed under the "Additional Billing" section of production licenses. It is the licensee's responsibility to ensure any and all required billing is included in the requisite places, per the terms of the license.

SPECIAL NOTE ON SONGS AND RECORDINGS

For performances of copyrighted songs, arrangements or recordings mentioned in these Plays, the permission of the copyright owner(s) must be obtained. Other songs, arrangements or recordings may be substituted provided permission from the copyright owner(s) of such songs, arrangements or recordings is obtained; or songs, arrangements or recordings in the public domain may be substituted.

THE CURIOUS INCIDENT OF THE DOG IN THE NIGHT-TIME was first presented by the National Theatre in London at the Cottesloe Theatre on August 2, 2012, and transferred to the Gielgud Theatre, West End, on March 12, 2013. It was directed by Marianne Elliott; the set design was by Bunny Christie; the lighting design was by Paul Constable; the video design was by Finn Ross; the music was by Adrian Sutton; and the sound design was by Ian Dickinson. The cast was as follows:

CHRISTOPHER .... Luke Treadaway
SIOBHAN .... Niamh Cusack
ED .... Paul Ritter
JUDY .... Nicola Walker
VOICE ONE/MRS. SHEARS (and others) .... Sophie Duval
VOICE TWO/ROGER SHEARS (and others) .... Nick Sidi
VOICE THREE/POLICEMAN (and others) .... Matthew Barker
VOICE FOUR/REV. PETERS (and others) .... Howard Ward
VOICE FIVE/NO. 40 (and others) .... Rhiannon Harper-Rafferty
VOICE SIX/MRS. ALEXANDER (and others) .... Una Stubbs

The National Theatre production of THE CURIOUS INCIDENT OF THE DOG IN THE NIGHT-TIME opened on Broadway at the Ethel Barrymore Theatre on October 5, 2014, with the same creative team. The cast was as follows:

CHRISTOPHER .... Alex Sharp (Taylor Trensch, alternate)
SIOBHAN .... Francesca Faridany
ED .... Ian Barford
JUDY .... Enid Graham
VOICE ONE/MRS. SHEARS (and others) ..... Mercedes Herrero
VOICE TWO/ROGER SHEARS (and others) ..... Richard Hollis
VOICE THREE/POLICEMAN (and others) .... Ben Horner
VOICE FOUR/REV. PETERS (and others) .... David Manis
VOICE FIVE/NO. 40 (and others) .... Jocelyn Bioh
VOICE SIX/MRS. ALEXANDER (and others) .... Helen Carey

CHARACTERS

CHRISTOPHER

SIOBHAN

ED

JUDY

COMPANY DOUBLING

VOICE ONE, MRS. SHEARS, MRS. GASCOYNE, WOMAN ON TRAIN, SHOPKEEPER

VOICE TWO, ROGER (MR. SHEARS), DUTY SERGEANT, MR. WISE, MAN BEHIND COUNTER, DRUNK ONE

VOICE THREE, POLICEMAN, MR. THOMPSON, DRUNK TWO, MAN WITH SOCKS, LONDON POLICEMAN

VOICE FOUR, REVEREND PETERS, UNCLE TERRY, STATION POLICEMAN, STATION GUARD

VOICE FIVE, NO. 40, LADY IN STREET, INFORMATION, PUNK GIRL

VOICE SIX, MRS. ALEXANDER, POSH WOMAN

NOTES

All actors remain onstage unless prescribed otherwise.

There is also a dead dog. With a garden fork sticking out of it.

Scenes run into one another without interruption regardless of alterations in space or time or chronology.

THE CURIOUS INCIDENT OF THE DOG IN THE NIGHT-TIME

PART ONE

1. GARDEN

A dead dog lies in the middle of the stage. A large garden fork is sticking out of its side.
Christopher Boone, 15 years old, stands on one side of it. His 42-year-old neighbour Mrs. Shears stands on the other.
They stand for a while without saying anything. The rest of the company watch, waiting to see who is going to dare to speak first.

MRS. SHEARS. Holy fuck. What have you done?
   Christopher is frozen to the spot.
Oh no. Oh my fucking Christ.
   Christopher's teacher, Siobhan, opens Christopher's book. She reads from it.
SIOBHAN. "It was 7 minutes after midnight. The dog was lying on the grass in the middle of the lawn in front of Mrs. Shears' house.
Its eyes were closed. It looked as if it was running on its side, the way dogs run when they think they are chasing a cat in a dream. But the dog was not running or asleep. The dog was dead."
MRS. SHEARS. Get away from my dog.
SIOBHAN. "There was a garden fork sticking out of the dog. The dog was called Wellington. It belonged to Mrs. Shears who was

our friend. She lived on the opposite side of the road, 2 houses to the left."

MRS. SHEARS. Get away from my dog.

Christopher takes two steps away from the dog.

SIOBHAN. "My name is Christopher John Francis Boone. I live at 36 Randolph Street, Swindon, Wiltshire. I know all the countries of the world and capital cities. And every prime number up to 7,507."

MRS. SHEARS. Get away from my dog for Christ's sake.

Christopher puts his hands over his ears. He closes his eyes. He rolls forward. He presses his forehead onto the grass. He starts groaning.

SIOBHAN. "After 12 and a half minutes a policeman arrived. He had a big orange leaf stuck to the bottom of his shoe which was poking out from one side." This is good Christopher. It's quite exciting. I like the details. They make it more realistic.

A policeman enters. He has a big orange leaf stuck to the bottom of his shoe, which is poking out to one side. He squats next to Christopher.

"He squatted down next to me. He said to me:"

Christopher stops groaning.

POLICEMAN. Would you like to tell me what's going on here, young man?

Christopher lifts his head from the ground.
There is some time.
Christopher looks at the policeman.
There is some time.

SIOBHAN. "I do not tell lies. Mother used to say that this was because I was a good person. But it is not because I am a good person. It is because I can't tell lies."

CHRISTOPHER. The dog is dead.

POLICEMAN. I'd got that far.

CHRISTOPHER. I think someone killed the dog.

POLICEMAN. How old are you?

CHRISTOPHER. I'm 15 years and 3 months and 2 days.

POLICEMAN. And what precisely are you doing in the garden?

CHRISTOPHER. I'm talking to you.

POLICEMAN. OK, why were you in the garden in the first place?

CHRISTOPHER. I was holding the dog.

POLICEMAN. Why were you holding the dog?

CHRISTOPHER. I like dogs.

POLICEMAN. Did you kill the dog?

CHRISTOPHER. I did not kill the dog.
POLICEMAN. You seem very upset about this.
I'm going to ask you once again.
> *Christopher starts groaning.*

Terrific.
> *Christopher carries on groaning.*

Young man I'm going to ask you to stop making that noise and to stand up please calmly and quietly.
> *Christopher carries on groaning.*

Marvellous. Great. Just flipping —
> *The policeman tries to lift him up by his arm.*
> *Christopher screams. He hits the policeman.*
> *The policeman stares at Christopher. For a while the two look at one another, neither entirely sure what to say or quite believing what has just happened.*

I'm arresting you for assaulting a police officer. I strongly advise you to get into the back of the police car because if you try any of that monkey business again you stupid idiot I am going to seriously lose my shit. Is that understood?

2. SCHOOL

SIOBHAN. "I find people confusing. This is for two main reasons. The first main reason is that people do a lot of talking without using any words. Siobhan says that if you raise one eyebrow it can mean lots of different things. It can mean 'I want to do sex with you.'" I never said that.
CHRISTOPHER. Yes you did.
SIOBHAN. I didn't use those words Christopher.
CHRISTOPHER. You did on September 12th last year. At first break.
SIOBHAN. "And it can also mean 'I think that what you just said was very stupid.'"

3. POLICE STATION

DUTY SERGEANT. Could you empty your pockets onto the desk, please?

CHRISTOPHER. Is that in case I have anything in them that I could use to kill myself or escape or attack a policeman with?

The duty sergeant looks at him for a beat.

DUTY SERGEANT. That's right.

CHRISTOPHER. I've got a Swiss Army knife but I only use that for doing "odd jobs," not for stabbing things or hurting people.

DUTY SERGEANT. Jolly good.

Christopher empties his pockets.

VOICE FOUR. A piece of string.

VOICE FIVE. A piece of a wooden puzzle.

VOICE SIX. 3 pellets of rat food for Toby, my pet rat.

VOICE FOUR. 1 pound 47 (this was made up of a 1-pound coin, a 20p coin, 2 10p coins, a 5p coin, and a 2p coin).

VOICE SIX. A red paper clip.

VOICE FOUR. A key for the front door.

VOICE FIVE. A Swiss Army knife with 13 attachments, including a wire-stripper and a saw and a toothpick and tweezers.

DUTY SERGEANT. Could you take your watch off please Christopher?

CHRISTOPHER. No.

DUTY SERGEANT. I'm sorry Christopher?

CHRISTOPHER. I need my watch to know exactly what time it is.

DUTY SERGEANT. Give it here lad.

Christopher screams.

All right, son, you keep it. Do you have any family Christopher?

CHRISTOPHER. Yes I do.

DUTY SERGEANT. And who is your family.

CHRISTOPHER. Father and Mother but Mother is dead. And also Uncle Terry who is in Sunderland. He is my father's brother. And my grandparents too but 3 of them are dead and Grandma Burton is in a home because she has senile dementia and thinks I'm someone on television.

DUTY SERGEANT. Right. Lovely. Do you know your father's phone number Christopher?

4. POLICE STATION

Christopher turns to Ed. Ed looks at him. Ed holds his hand out in front of him with his fingers stretched. Christopher does the same. They touch fingers. Then let go.

CHRISTOPHER. I could see the Milky Way as they drove me towards the town centre.

ED. Could you?

CHRISTOPHER. Some people think the Milky Way is a long line of stars, but it isn't. Our galaxy is a huge disc of stars millions of light-years across.

For a long time scientists were puzzled by the fact that the sky is dark at night even though there are billions of stars in the universe.

ED. Is that right?

DUTY SERGEANT. Christopher. Mr. Boone. Could you come this way please?

CHRISTOPHER. Are you going to interview me and record the interview?

DUTY SERGEANT. I don't think there will be any need for that.

I've spoken to your father and he says you didn't mean to hit the policeman. Did you mean to hit the policeman?

CHRISTOPHER. Yes.

DUTY SERGEANT. But you didn't mean to hurt the policeman?

CHRISTOPHER. No. I didn't mean to hurt the policeman, I just wanted him to stop touching me.

DUTY SERGEANT. You know that it's wrong to hit a policeman don't you?

CHRISTOPHER. I do.

DUTY SERGEANT. Did you kill the dog Christopher?

CHRISTOPHER. I did not kill the dog.

DUTY SERGEANT. Do you know that it is wrong to lie to a police-man and that you can get into a very great deal of trouble if you do?

CHRISTOPHER. Yes.

DUTY SERGEANT. Do you know who killed the dog?

CHRISTOPHER. No.

DUTY SERGEANT. Are you telling the truth?

CHRISTOPHER. Yes. I always tell the truth.

DUTY SERGEANT. Right. I'm going to give you a caution.

CHRISTOPHER. Is that going to be on a piece of paper like a certificate I can keep?

DUTY SERGEANT. No. A caution means that we are going to keep a record of what you did, that you hit a policeman but that it was an accident and that you didn't mean to hurt the policeman.

CHRISTOPHER. But it wasn't an accident.

ED. Christopher, please.

DUTY SERGEANT. If you get into any more trouble we will take out this record and see that you have been given a caution and we will take things much more seriously. Do you understand what I'm saying?

CHRISTOPHER. Yes.

5. SCHOOL

SIOBHAN. "The second main reason I find people confusing is that people often talk using metaphors. These are examples of metaphors:"

VOICE THREE. I am going to seriously lose my shit.

VOICE FOUR. He was the apple of her eye.

VOICE THREE. They had a skeleton in the cupboard.

VOICE ONE. We had a real pig of a day.

VOICE TWO. The dog was stone dead.

SIOBHAN. "The word metaphor means carrying something from one place to another and it is when you describe something by using a word for something that it isn't. This means that the word metaphor is a metaphor." Wow. That's clever.

CHRISTOPHER. It's true.

SIOBHAN. Yes. "I think it should be called a lie because a pig is not like a day and people do not have skeletons in their cupboards. And when I try and make a picture of the phrase in my head it just confuses me because imagining an apple in someone's eye doesn't have anything to do with liking someone a lot and it makes you forget what the person was talking about."

6. HOME

Christopher turns to Ed.

CHRISTOPHER. I'm sorry.
ED. It's OK.
CHRISTOPHER. I didn't kill Wellington.
ED. I know.
Christopher you have to stay out of trouble, OK?
CHRISTOPHER. I didn't know I was going to get into trouble. I like Wellington and I went to say hello to him, but I didn't know that someone had killed him.
ED. Just try and keep your nose out of other people's business.
CHRISTOPHER. I am going to find out who killed Wellington.
ED. Were you listening to what I was saying, Christopher?
CHRISTOPHER. Yes I was listening to what you were saying but when someone gets murdered you have to find out who did it so that they can be punished.
ED. It's a bloody dog, Christopher, a bloody dog.
CHRISTOPHER. I think dogs are important too. I think some dogs are cleverer than some people. Nicholas, for example, who comes to school on Thursdays needs help eating his food and he probably couldn't even fetch a stick.
ED. Leave it.
CHRISTOPHER. I wonder if the police will find out who killed him and punish the person.
ED. I said leave it for God's sake.
CHRISTOPHER. Are you sad about Wellington?
ED. Yes Christopher you could say that. You could very well say that.

7. HOME

SIOBHAN. *(Reads more from the book.)* "Mother died 2 years ago. I came home from school one day and no one answered the door, so I went and found the secret key that we keep under a flowerpot outside the kitchen window. I let myself into the house and wiped my feet on the mat. I put the key in the bowl on the table. I took my coat off and hung it by the side of the fridge so it would be ready for school the next day and gave 3 pellets of rat food to Toby who is my pet rat. I made myself a raspberry milkshake and heated it up in the microwave. Then I went up to my bedroom and turned on my bedroom light and played 6 games of Tetris and got to level 38 which is my 4th best-ever score. An hour later Father came home from work."

ED. Christopher have you seen your mum?

CHRISTOPHER. No.

SIOBHAN. "He went downstairs and started making some phone calls. I did not hear what he said. Then he came up to my room and said he had to go out for a while and he wasn't sure how long he would be. He said that if I needed anything I should call him on his mobile phone.

He was away for 2 and a half hours. When he came back I went downstairs."

ED. I'm afraid you won't be seeing your mother for a while.

CHRISTOPHER. Why not?

ED. Your mother has had to go into hospital.

CHRISTOPHER. Can we visit her?

ED. No.

CHRISTOPHER. Why can't we?

ED. She needs rest. She needs to be on her own.

CHRISTOPHER. Is it a psychiatric hospital?

ED. No. It's an ordinary hospital. She has a problem ... a problem with her heart.

CHRISTOPHER. I'll make her a get-well card.

If I make her a get-well card, will you take it in for her tomorrow?

8. SCHOOL

SIOBHAN. How are you today Christopher?

CHRISTOPHER. I'm very well thank you.

SIOBHAN. That's good.

CHRISTOPHER. In the bus on the way to school we passed 4 red cars in a row.

SIOBHAN. 4?

CHRISTOPHER. So today is a Good Day.

SIOBHAN. Great. I am glad.

CHRISTOPHER. I've decided I am going to try and find out who killed Wellington because a Good Day is a day for projects and planning things.

SIOBHAN. Who's Wellington?

CHRISTOPHER. Wellington is a dog that used to belong to my neighbour Mrs. Shears who is our friend, but he is dead now because somebody killed him by putting a garden fork through him. And I found him and then a policeman thought I'd killed him but I hadn't and then he tried to touch me so I hit him and then I had to go to the police station.

SIOBHAN. Gosh.

CHRISTOPHER. And I am going to find out who really killed Wellington and make it a project. Even though Father told me not to.

SIOBHAN. Did he?

CHRISTOPHER. Yes.

SIOBHAN. I see.

CHRISTOPHER. I don't always do what I'm told.

SIOBHAN. Why?

CHRISTOPHER. Because when people tell you what to do it is usually confusing and does not make sense. For example people often say "Be quiet" but they don't tell you how long to be quiet for.

SIOBHAN. No. Why did your father tell you not to try to find out who killed Wellington?

CHRISTOPHER. I don't know.

SIOBHAN. If your father's told you not to do something maybe you shouldn't do it.

CHRISTOPHER. Mmm.

SIOBHAN. Well, we're meant to be writing stories today, so why don't you write about what happened to Wellington?
CHRISTOPHER. OK, I will.

9. HOME

ED. Christopher I'm sorry, your mother's died.
She's had a heart attack.
It wasn't expected.
CHRISTOPHER. What kind of heart attack?
ED. I don't know what kind of heart attack. Now isn't the moment Christopher to be asking questions like that.
CHRISTOPHER. It was probably an aneurysm.
ED. I'm sorry Christopher, I'm really sorry.

10. STREET

Mrs. Shears' house is assembled.

SIOBHAN. "That evening I went round to Mrs. Shears' house and knocked on the door and waited for her to answer it."
Mrs. Shears answers her door. She is drinking a cup of tea.
MRS. SHEARS. What are you doing here?
CHRISTOPHER. I wanted to come and tell you that I didn't kill Wellington. And also I want to find out who killed him.
MRS. SHEARS. Christopher, I really don't think I want to see you right now.
CHRISTOPHER. Do you know who killed Wellington?
MRS. SHEARS. If you don't go now I will call the police again.

11. SCHOOL

CHRISTOPHER. Reverend Peters, where is heaven?

REVEREND PETERS. I'm sorry Christopher?

CHRISTOPHER. In our universe whereabouts is it exactly?

REVEREND PETERS. It's not in our universe. It's another kind of place altogether.

CHRISTOPHER. There isn't anything outside our universe Reverend Peters. There isn't another kind of place altogether. Except there might be if you go through a black hole. But a black hole is what is called a Singularity which means it's impossible to find out what is on the other side because the gravity of a black hole is so big that even electromagnetic waves like light can't get out of it, and electromagnetic waves are how we get information about things which are far away. And if heaven is on the other side of a black hole then dead people would have to be fired into space on a rocket to get there and they aren't or people would notice.

Reverend Peters looks at him for a while before he responds.

REVEREND PETERS. Well when I say heaven is outside our universe it's really just a manner of speaking. I suppose what it really means is that they are with God.

CHRISTOPHER. But where is God?

REVEREND PETERS. Christopher we should talk about this on another day when I have more time.

12. STREET

SIOBHAN. "The next day was Saturday and there is not much to do on a Saturday unless Father takes me out somewhere on an outing to the boating lake or to the garden centre, but on this Saturday England were playing Romania at football which meant that we weren't going to go on an outing because Father wanted to watch the match on the television. So I made a decision. I decided to do some more detection. I decided to go out on my own. I do not like strangers. So talking to the other people in our street was brave. But if you are going to do detective work you have to be brave, so I had no choice."

MR. THOMPSON. Can I help you?

CHRISTOPHER. Do you know who killed Wellington?

MR. THOMPSON. Who are you?

CHRISTOPHER. I'm Christopher Boone from number 36 and I know you. You're Mr. Thompson.

MR. THOMPSON. I'm Mr. Thompson's brother.

CHRISTOPHER. Do you know who killed Wellington?

MR. THOMPSON. Who the hell is Wellington?

CHRISTOPHER. Mrs. Shears' dog. Mrs. Shears is from number 39.

MR. THOMPSON. Someone killed her dog?

CHRISTOPHER. With a fork.

MR. THOMPSON. Jesus Christ.

CHRISTOPHER. A garden fork.

MR. THOMPSON. Oh.

CHRISTOPHER. Do you know who killed him?

MR. THOMPSON. I haven't a bloody clue.

CHRISTOPHER. Did you see anything suspicious on Thursday evening?

MR. THOMPSON. Look son, do you really think you should be going round asking questions like this?

CHRISTOPHER. Yes I do, because I want to find out who killed Wellington and I am writing a book about it.

MR. THOMPSON. Well I was in Colchester on Thursday so you're asking the wrong bloke.

CHRISTOPHER. Thank you for helping with my investigation.

NO. 40. It's Christopher isn't it?

CHRISTOPHER. Yes it is. Do you know who killed Wellington?

NO. 40. No. No. I don't. No. I'm sorry.

CHRISTOPHER. Did you see anything suspicious on Thursday evening, which might be a clue?

NO. 40. Like what?

CHRISTOPHER. Like strangers or the sound of people arguing.

NO. 40. Perhaps you should be talking to your father about this.

CHRISTOPHER. I can't talk to my father about it because he told me to stay out of other people's business.

NO. 40. Well maybe he has a point Christopher.

CHRISTOPHER. So you don't know anything that might be a clue.

NO. 40. No. You be careful, young man.

CHRISTOPHER. I will be. Thank you for helping me with my investigation.

Do you know who killed Wellington?

MR. WISE. Bloody hell. Policemen really are getting younger aren't they?

Mr. Wise laughs. Christopher walks away.

CHRISTOPHER. 2, 3, 5, 7, 11, 13, 17, 19, 23, 29, 31, 37, 41, 43, 47, 53, 59, 61, 67, 71, 73, 79, 83, 89, 97

Do you know anything about Wellington getting killed?

MRS. ALEXANDER. I heard about it yesterday. Dreadful. Dreadful.

CHRISTOPHER. Do you know who killed him?

MRS. ALEXANDER. No, I don't.

CHRISTOPHER. Somebody must know because the person who killed Wellington knows that they killed Wellington. Unless they were a loony person and didn't know what they were doing. Or unless they had amnesia.

MRS. ALEXANDER. You're Christopher aren't you?

CHRISTOPHER. Yes. I live at number 36.

MRS. ALEXANDER. We haven't talked before, have we?

CHRISTOPHER. No. I don't talk to strangers. But I'm doing detective work.

MRS. ALEXANDER. I see you every day, going to school on your school bus, when I'm walking my dog. It's very nice of you to come and say hello. Even if it's only because you're doing detective work.

CHRISTOPHER. Thank you.

MRS. ALEXANDER. I have a grandson your age.

CHRISTOPHER. My age is 15 years and 3 months and 3 days.

MRS. ALEXANDER. Well, almost your age. You don't have a dog, do you?

CHRISTOPHER. No.

MRS. ALEXANDER. You'd probably like a dog wouldn't you?

CHRISTOPHER. I have a rat.

MRS. ALEXANDER. A rat?

CHRISTOPHER. He's called Toby.

MRS. ALEXANDER. Oh.

CHRISTOPHER. Most people don't like rats because they think they carry diseases like bubonic plague. But that's only because they lived in sewers and stowed away on ships coming from foreign countries where there were strange diseases. But rats are very clean.

MRS. ALEXANDER. Do you want to come in for tea?

CHRISTOPHER. I don't go into other people's houses.

MRS. ALEXANDER. Well, maybe I could bring some tea out here. Do you like lemonade?

CHRISTOPHER. I only like orangeade.

MRS. ALEXANDER. Luckily I have some of that as well. And what about Battenberg?

CHRISTOPHER. I don't know because I don't know what Battenberg is.

MRS. ALEXANDER. It's a type of cake. It has marzipan icing round the edge.

CHRISTOPHER. Is it a long cake with a square cross-section that can be divided into equally sized, alternately coloured squares?

MRS. ALEXANDER. Yes I think you could probably describe it like that.

CHRISTOPHER. I think I'd like the pink squares but not the yellow squares because I don't like yellow. And I don't know what marzipan is so I don't know whether I'll like that.

MRS. ALEXANDER. I'm afraid marzipan is yellow too. Perhaps I should bring out some cookies instead. Do you like cookies?

CHRISTOPHER. Yes. Some sorts of cookies.

MRS. ALEXANDER. I'll get a selection.

> *She goes into her house.*
> *He waits. Then before she gets back:*

13. SCHOOL

SIOBHAN. "She moved very slowly because she was an old lady and she was inside the house for more than 6 minutes and I began to get nervous because I didn't know her well enough to know whether she was telling the truth about getting orangeade and Battenberg cake. And I thought she might be ringing the police and then I'd get into much more serious trouble because of the caution. So I walked away."

> *The company cheer, as if a goal has been scored.*

CHRISTOPHER. Why would you kill a dog?

SIOBHAN. I wouldn't.

CHRISTOPHER. I think you would only kill a dog if (a) you hated the dog or (b) if you were a lunatic or (c) because you wanted to make Mrs. Shears sad. I don't know anybody who hated Wellington so if it was (a) it was probably a stranger. I don't know any lunatics either, so if it was (b) it was also probably a stranger.

SIOBHAN. Right.

CHRISTOPHER. But most murders are committed by someone who is known to the victim. In fact, you are most likely to be murdered by a member of your own family on Christmas Day.

SIOBHAN. Is that a fact?

CHRISTOPHER. Yes actually it is a fact. Wellington was therefore most likely to have been killed by someone known to him. I only know one person who didn't like Mrs. Shears and that is Mr. Shears who divorced Mrs. Shears and left her to live somewhere else and who knew Wellington very well indeed. This means that Mr. Shears is my Prime Suspect.

SIOBHAN. Christopher —

CHRISTOPHER. I am going to find out more about Mr. Shears.

14. SCHOOL OFFICE

MRS. GASCOYNE. Mr. Boone, nobody has ever taken an A-level examination in the school before.

ED. He can be the first then.

MRS. GASCOYNE. I don't know if we have the facilities in the school to allow him to do that.

ED. Then get the facilities.

MRS. GASCOYNE. I can't treat Christopher differently to any other student.

ED. Why not?

MRS. GASCOYNE. Because then everybody would want to be treated differently.

ED. So?

MRS. GASCOYNE. It would set a precedent. Christopher can always do his A-levels later. When he's 18. Which is, after all, the age everyone else takes their A-levels.

ED. Christopher is getting a crap enough deal already don't you think, without you shitting on him from a great height as well. Jesus, this is the one thing he's really good at.

MRS. GASCOYNE. We should talk about this later. Maybe on our own.

ED. Are there things which you're too embarrassed to say to me in front of Christopher?

MRS. GASCOYNE. No. It's not that.

ED. Say them now then.

MRS. GASCOYNE. If Christopher takes an A-level then he would have to have a member of staff, a supervisor, looking after him on his own in a separate room.

ED. I'll pay for it. They can do it after school. Here. 50 quid. Is that enough?

MRS. GASCOYNE. Mr. Boone.

ED. I'm not going to take no for an answer.

Ed turns to Christopher.

15. HOME

ED. Where have you been?

CHRISTOPHER. I have been out.

ED. I have just had a phone call from Mrs. Shears. What the hell were you doing poking round her garden?

CHRISTOPHER. I was doing detective work trying to figure out who killed Wellington.

ED. How many times do I have to tell you Christopher? I told you to keep your nose out of other people's business.

CHRISTOPHER. I think Mr. Shears probably killed Wellington.

ED. *(Shouts.)* I will not have that man's name mentioned in my house.

Beat.

Everybody onstage pauses to look at Ed and Christopher.

CHRISTOPHER. Why not?

ED. That man is evil.

CHRISTOPHER. Does that mean he might have killed Wellington?

ED. Jesus wept. OK Christopher. I am going to say this for the last and final time. I will not tell you again. Look at me when I'm talking to you for God's sake. Look at me. You are not to go asking Mrs. Shears who killed that bloody dog. You are not to go asking anyone who killed that bloody dog. You are not to go trespassing on other people's gardens. You are to stop this ridiculous bloody detective game right now. I am going to make you promise me Christopher. And you know what it means when I make you promise.

16. HOME

SIOBHAN. "I think I would make a very good astronaut."

ED. Yes mate. You probably would.

SIOBHAN. "To be a good astronaut you have to be intelligent and I'm intelligent. You also have to understand how machines work and I'm good at understanding how machines work."

CHRISTOPHER. You also have to be someone who would like being on their own in a tiny spacecraft thousands and thousands of miles away from the surface of the Earth and not panic or get claustrophobia or homesick or insane. And I really like little spaces so long as there is no one else in them with me.

ED. I noticed.

SIOBHAN. "Sometimes when I want to be on my own I get into the laundry room and slide in beside the boiler and pull the door closed behind me and sit there and think for hours and it makes me feel very calm."

CHRISTOPHER. So I would have to be an astronaut on my own or have my own part of the spacecraft that no one else could come into.

And also there are no yellow things or brown things in a spacecraft so that would be OK, too.

And I would have to talk to other people from Mission Control, but we would do that through a radio link-up and a TV monitor so it wouldn't be like real people who are strangers but it would be like playing a computer game.

ED. Which you like.

CHRISTOPHER. Also I wouldn't be homesick at all because I'd be surrounded by lots of things I like, which are machines and computers and outer space. And I would be able to look out of a little window in the spacecraft and know that there was no one else near me for thousands and thousands —

ED. Christopher.

CHRISTOPHER. What?

ED. Could you please, just, give it a bit of a break, mate. Please.

SIOBHAN. "And know that there was no one else near me for thousands and thousands of miles which is what I sometimes pretend at night in the summer when I go and lie on the lawn and look up at the sky and I put my hands round the sides of my face so that I can't see the fence and the chimney and the clothes line and I can pretend I'm in space.

And all I could see would be stars. And stars are the places where the molecules that life is made of were constructed billions of years ago. For example, all the iron in your blood, which stops you being anaemic, was made in a star.

And I would like it if I could take Toby with me into space, and that might be allowed because they sometimes do take animals into space for experiments, so if I could think of a good experiment you could do with a rat that didn't hurt the rat, I could make them let me take Toby. But if they didn't let me I would still go because it would be a Dream Come True."

17. SCHOOL

CHRISTOPHER. Father said.

SIOBHAN. I see, that's a pity.

CHRISTOPHER. So the book is finished.

SIOBHAN. Well, Christopher, if your father said he wanted you to stop then I think he probably has a good reason and I think you should stop. But you can still be very proud because what you've written so far is just, well, it's great.

CHRISTOPHER. It's not a proper book.

SIOBHAN. Why not?

CHRISTOPHER. It doesn't have a proper ending. I never found out who killed Wellington. So the murderer is still At Large.

SIOBHAN. Not all murders are solved. Not all murderers are caught.

CHRISTOPHER. Father said I was never to mention Mr. Shears' name in our house again and that he was an evil man and maybe that meant he was the person who killed Wellington.

SIOBHAN. I think you should do what your father tells you to do.

18. THE STREET

MRS. ALEXANDER. What happened to you the other day? I came out again and you'd gone. I had to eat all the biscuits myself. I was looking forward to our little chat.

CHRISTOPHER. I don't do chatting. I don't like it.

MRS. ALEXANDER. No, I don't suppose you do. Do you like computers?

CHRISTOPHER. Yes, I like computers. I have a computer in my room.

MRS. ALEXANDER. I know. I can see you sitting at your computer in your bedroom sometimes when I look across the street.

CHRISTOPHER. And I like maths and looking after Toby. And I also like outer space and I like being on my own.

MRS. ALEXANDER. I bet you're very good at maths aren't you?

CHRISTOPHER. I am. I'm going to do A-level maths next month. And I'm going to get an A-star.

MRS. ALEXANDER. Really? A-level maths?

CHRISTOPHER. I'm the first person to take an A-level from my school because it's a special school. All the other children at my school are stupid. Except I'm not meant to call them that, even though that is what they are.

MRS. ALEXANDER. Well I am very impressed. And I hope you do get an A-star.

CHRISTOPHER. I will.

MRS. ALEXANDER. And the other thing I know about you is your favourite colour is not yellow.

CHRISTOPHER. No. And it's not brown either. My favourite colour is red and metal-colour. Do you know Mr. Shears?

MRS. ALEXANDER. Not really, no. I mean I knew him well enough to say hello but I didn't know much about him. I think he worked in the National Westminster Bank in town.

CHRISTOPHER. Father said that he is an evil man. Do you know why he said that?

MRS. ALEXANDER. Perhaps it would be best not to talk about these things Christopher.

CHRISTOPHER. Why not?

MRS. ALEXANDER. Because maybe your father is right and you shouldn't go round asking questions about this.

CHRISTOPHER. Why?

MRS. ALEXANDER. Because obviously he is going to find it quite upsetting.

CHRISTOPHER. Why is he going to find it quite upsetting?

MRS. ALEXANDER. I think you know why your father doesn't like Mr. Shears very much.

CHRISTOPHER. Did Mr. Shears kill Mother?

MRS. ALEXANDER. Kill her?

CHRISTOPHER. Yes. Did he kill Mother?

MRS. ALEXANDER. No. No. Of course he didn't kill your mother.

CHRISTOPHER. But did he give her stress so that she died of a heart attack?

MRS. ALEXANDER. I honestly don't know what you're talking about, Christopher.

CHRISTOPHER. Or did he hurt her so that she had to go into hospital?

MRS. ALEXANDER. Did she have to go into hospital?

CHRISTOPHER. Yes. And it wasn't very serious at first but she had a heart attack when she was in hospital.

MRS. ALEXANDER. Oh my goodness.

CHRISTOPHER. And she died.

MRS. ALEXANDER. Oh my goodness. Oh Christopher, I am so, so sorry. I never realised.

CHRISTOPHER. Why did you say "I think you know why your father doesn't like Mr. Shears very much"?

MRS. ALEXANDER. Oh dear, dear, dear. Christopher look, perhaps we should take a little walk in the park together. This is not the place to be talking about this kind of thing.

19. PARK

MRS. ALEXANDER. I am going to say something to you and you must promise not to tell your father that I told you this.

CHRISTOPHER. Why?

MRS. ALEXANDER. Christopher, please, just trust me.

CHRISTOPHER. I promise.

MRS. ALEXANDER. Your mother before she died was very good friends with Mr. Shears.

CHRISTOPHER. I know.

MRS. ALEXANDER. No Christopher, I'm not sure that you do. I mean that they were very good friends. Very, very good friends.

CHRISTOPHER. Do you mean that they were doing sex?

MRS. ALEXANDER. Yes, Christopher. That is what I mean. I'm sorry Christopher. I really didn't mean to say anything that was going to upset you.

CHRISTOPHER. Was that why Mr. Shears left Mrs. Shears, because he was doing sex with someone else when he was still married to Mrs. Shears?

MRS. ALEXANDER. Yes. I expect so.

CHRISTOPHER. I think I should go now.

MRS. ALEXANDER. Are you OK Christopher?

CHRISTOPHER. I can't be on my own with you because you are a stranger.

MRS. ALEXANDER. I'm not a stranger Christopher, I'm a friend.

20. SCHOOL

Ed finds Christopher's book on the kitchen table.

SIOBHAN. Have you told your father about this?

CHRISTOPHER. No.

SIOBHAN. Are you going to tell your father about this?

CHRISTOPHER. No.

> *Ed goes to the book.*
> *There is a tone.*
> *He begins reading Christopher's book.*

SIOBHAN. Did it make you sad to find this out?

CHRISTOPHER. Find what out?

SIOBHAN. Did it make you sad to find out that your mother and Mr. Shears had an affair?

CHRISTOPHER. No.

SIOBHAN. Are you telling the truth?

CHRISTOPHER. Yes, I always tell the truth. It didn't make me feel sad because Mother is dead. So I would be feeling sad about something that isn't real and doesn't exist and that would be stupid.

SIOBHAN. What was your mother like?

Do you remember much about her?

CHRISTOPHER. I remember the 20th of July 2008. I was 9 years old. It was a Sunday. We were on holiday in Cornwall. We were on the beach in a place called Polperro. Mother was wearing a pair of shorts made out of denim and a stripy blue swimming costume, and she was smoking menthol cigarettes, which were mint flavour. And she wasn't swimming. She was sunbathing on a towel, which had red and purple stripes, and she was reading a book by Georgette Heyer called *The Masqueraders*. And then she finished sunbathing and went into the water and she said:

JUDY. Bloody Nora it's cold.

21. BEACH

CHRISTOPHER. "Bloody Nora it's cold." And she said I should come and swim too, but I didn't like swimming because I don't like taking my clothes off. And she said I should just roll my trousers up and walk into the water a little way. So I did. And Mother said:

JUDY. Christopher! Look, it's lovely.

CHRISTOPHER. And she jumped backwards and disappeared under the water and I thought a shark had eaten her and I screamed. And she stood up out of the water and came over to where I was standing and held up her right hand and spread out her fingers like a fan.

JUDY. Come on Christopher, touch my hand. Come on now. Stop screaming. Touch my hand. Listen to me Christopher. You can do it. It's OK Christopher. It's OK. There aren't any sharks in Cornwall.

ED. "When we were inside the park Mrs. Alexander stopped walking and said 'I am going to say something to you and you must promise not to tell your father that I told you this. Your mother before she died was very good friends with Mr. Shears.'"

CHRISTOPHER. And other times she used to say:

JUDY. If I hadn't married your father I think I'd be living in a little farmhouse in the South of France with someone called Jean. And he'd be, ooh, a local handyman. You know, doing painting and decorating for people, gardening, building fences. And we'd have a French bulldog. And a veranda with figs growing over it and there would be a field of sunflowers at the bottom of the garden and a little town on the hill in the distance and we'd sit outside in the evening and drink red wine and smoke French cigarettes and watch the sun go down.

22. HOME

ED. What is this?

Christopher looks at Ed.

CHRISTOPHER. It's a book I'm writing.

ED. Is this true? Did you speak to Mrs. Alexander?

CHRISTOPHER. Yes.

ED. Jesus, Christopher, how stupid are you? What did I tell you Christopher?

CHRISTOPHER. Not to mention Mr. Shears' name in our house. And not to go asking Mrs. Shears or anyone about who killed that bloody dog. And not to go trespassing on other people's gardens. And to stop this ridiculous bloody detective game. Except I haven't done any of those things. I just asked Mrs. Alexander about Mr. Shears because I was doing chatting.

ED. Don't give me that bollocks. You knew exactly what you were bloody doing. I've read the book, remember. What else did I say Christopher?

CHRISTOPHER. I don't know.

ED. Come on Memory Man. Not to go round sticking your nose into other people's business. And what do you do? You go around sticking your nose into other people's business. You go around digging up the past and sharing it with every Tom, Dick, and Harry you bump into. What am I going to do with you Christopher? What the fuck am I going to do with you?

Ed throws Christopher's book.

CHRISTOPHER. I was just chatting with Mrs. Alexander. I wasn't doing investigating.

ED. I ask you to do one thing for me, Christopher. One thing.
CHRISTOPHER. I didn't want to talk to Mrs. Alexander. It was Mrs. Alexander who …

> *Ed grabs Christopher's arm.*
> *Christopher screams.*
> *Ed and Christopher tussle.*
> *Ed hits Christopher hard.*
> *Christopher falls.*
> *Ed stands above him.*

ED. I need a drink.

> *He goes and picks up the book.*
> *He leaves.*
> *He comes back without the book.*

I'm sorry I hit you. I didn't mean to.
I love you very much Christopher. Don't ever forget that. I worry about you, because I don't want to see you getting into trouble, because I don't want you to get hurt.
CHRISTOPHER. Where's my book?
ED. Christopher, do you understand that I love you?

> *Ed holds his right hand up and spreads his fingers out in a fan.*
> *Christopher does the same with his left hand. They make their*
> *fingers and thumbs touch each other.*

CHRISTOPHER. Is it in the dustbin at the front of the house?

23. MAP OF HOUSE

SIOBHAN. "The next day, when I got home from school, Father was still at work so I went outside and looked inside the dustbin. But the book wasn't there.
I wondered if Father had put it into his van and driven to the dump and put it into one of the big bins there but I did not want that to be true because then I would never see it again. One other possibility was that Father had hidden my book somewhere in the house. So I decided to do some detecting and see if I could find it.
I started by looking in the kitchen.
Then I detected in the laundry room.
Then I detected in the dining room.

Then I detected in the living room where I found the missing wheel from my Airfix Messerschmitt Bf109G-6 model under the sofa.

Then I went upstairs but I didn't do any detecting in my own room because I reasoned that Father wouldn't hide something from me in my own room unless he was being very clever and doing what is called a Double Bluff like in a real murder-mystery novel, so I decided to look in my own room only if I couldn't find the book anywhere else.

I detected in the bathroom, but the only place to look was in the medicine cabinet and there was nothing in there.

Which meant the only room left to detect in was Father's bedroom. I started by looking under the bed.

There were 5 shoes and a comb with lots of hair in it and a monkey wrench and a chocolate chip cookie and a magazine called *Men Only* and a pair of underpants from TJ Maxx with a little bit of pee left in them and a Scooby-Doo tie and a wooden spoon, but not my book.

Then I looked in the drawers on either side of the dressing table. But these only contained aspirin and nail clippers and batteries and dental floss and tissues and a spare false tooth and a tampon but my book wasn't there either.

Then I looked in his wardrobe. In the bottom of the wardrobe was a large plastic toolbox, which was full of tools for 'DIY' which means doing-it-yourself, but I could see these without opening the box because it was made of transparent grey plastic. Then I saw that there was another box underneath the toolbox.

The other box was an old cardboard box that is called a shirt box because people used to buy shirts in them."

Christopher finds these things including, finally, the shirt box.

"And when I opened the shirt box I saw my book was inside it."

Christopher finds his book.

"Then I heard Father's van pulling up outside the house and I knew that I had to think fast and be clever.

I heard Father shutting the door of the van.

And that is when I saw the envelope.

It was an envelope addressed to me and it was lying under my book in the shirt box with some other envelopes. I picked it up."

Christopher finds the envelope.

"It had never been opened.

It said:"

JUDY. Christopher Boone, 36 Randolph Street, Swindon, Wiltshire.

SIOBHAN. "Then I noticed there were lots of envelopes and they were all addressed to me. And this was interesting and confusing. And then I noticed how the words Christopher and Swindon were written. They were written like this."

JUDY. Christopher. Swindon.

SIOBHAN. "I only know 3 people who do little circles instead of dots over the letter *i*. And one of them is Siobhan. And one of them was Mr. Loxley who used to teach at the school. And one of them was Mother."

24. BACK TO REALITY

ED. Christopher?

CHRISTOPHER. Hello.

ED. So what have you been up to young man?

CHRISTOPHER. Today we did Life Skills with Siobhan. Which was Using Money and Public Transport. And I had tomato soup for lunch and 3 apples. And I practised some maths in the afternoon and we went for a walk in the park with Mrs. Peters and collected leaves for making collages.

ED. Excellent, excellent. What do you fancy for chow tonight?

CHRISTOPHER. Baked beans and broccoli.

ED. I think that can be very easily arranged.

I'm just going to put those shelves up in the living room if that's all right with you. I'll make a bit of a racket I'm afraid so if you want to watch television we're going to have to shift it upstairs.

CHRISTOPHER. I'll go and be on my own in my room.

ED. Good man.

SIOBHAN. "So, I went into my room. And when I was in the room I shut the door and took out the envelope. I opened the envelope. Inside there was a letter. And this was what was written in the letter:"

JUDY. 451c Chapter Road, Willesden, London NW2 5NG. 0208 887 8907. Dear Christopher. I was looking through some old photos last night, which made me sad. Then I found a photo of you playing with the train set we bought for you a couple of Christmases ago. And that made me happy because it was one of the really good times we had together. Do you remember how you played with it all day and you refused to go to bed at night because you were still playing with it. We told you about train timetables and you made a train timetable and you made the train run on time. And there was a little wooden station, too, and we showed you how people who wanted to go on the train went to the station and bought a ticket and then got on a train? And you played with it for weeks and weeks and weeks. I liked remembering that a lot.

You haven't written to me yet, so I know that you are probably still angry with me. I'm sorry Christopher. But I still love you. I hope you don't stay angry with me forever. And I'd love it if you were able to write me a letter.

I think about you all the time.

Lots of love,

Your Mum.

SIOBHAN. "I was really confused. Mother had never written me a letter before. And Mother had never lived in London.

I looked at the front of the envelope and I saw there was a postmark and there was a date on the postmark, the 16th of October 2013, which meant that the letter was posted 18 months after Mother had died. When I started writing my book there was only one mystery to solve. Now there were two. I decided that I would not think about it any more that night because I didn't have enough information and could easily LEAP TO THE WRONG CONCLUSIONS."

He lies down on the floor. He curls himself up into a ball.

25. NIGHT

Night falls. Morning rises.

26. SCHOOL

The next day Christopher comes home from school.

ED. You're soaking.
CHRISTOPHER. Yes.

31

ED. Give me your coat I'll hang it up.

How was school?

CHRISTOPHER. It was good thank you. Joseph Fleming took his trousers off and went to the toilet all over the floor of the changing room and started to eat it, but Mr. Davis stopped him.

ED. Good old Mr. Davis eh?

CHRISTOPHER. Joseph eats everything.

ED. Does he?

CHRISTOPHER. He once ate one of the little blocks of blue disinfectant, which hang inside the toilets. And he once ate a 50-pound note from his mother's wallet. And he eats string and rubber bands and tissues and writing paper and paints and plastic forks. Also he bangs his chin and screams a lot.

ED. I know how he feels. Christopher I've got to go out.

CHRISTOPHER. Why?

ED. I've just had a call. There's a lady. Her cellar has flooded. I've got to go out and fix it.

CHRISTOPHER. Is it an emergency?

ED. Yes mate.

CHRISTOPHER. It is raining very heavily.

ED. It is.

CHRISTOPHER. The rain looks like white sparks.

ED. Christopher if I go out, will you be OK?

CHRISTOPHER. Yes, I will because there's no one around because everybody's staying indoors.

ED. Good. Good. Good. Good lad.

CHRISTOPHER. I like looking at the rain.

ED. Terrific.

CHRISTOPHER. I like it because it makes me think how all the water in the world is connected.

ED. Does it?

CHRISTOPHER. This water, this rain has evaporated actually from somewhere like maybe the Gulf of Mexico maybe or Baffin Bay and now it's falling in front of the house.

ED. I'll have my mobile with me.

CHRISTOPHER. Yes.

ED. So you can call me if there's a problem.

CHRISTOPHER. Yes.

ED. Behave yourself Christopher yeah?

CHRISTOPHER. Yeah.

Ed exits.

SIOBHAN. "So I went into his bedroom and opened up the wardrobe and lifted the toolbox off the top of the shirt box and opened the shirt box. I counted out the letters. There were 43 of them. They were all addressed to me in the same handwriting. I took one and opened it. Inside was this letter:"

As Judy reads so Christopher begins to assemble his train set. His building becomes frantic. At times almost balletic.

JUDY. 451c Chapter Road, London, NW2 5NG. 0208 887 8907.

Dear Christopher. I said that I wanted to explain to you why I went away when I had the time to do it properly. Now I have lots of time. So I'm sitting on the sofa here with this letter and the radio on and I'm going to try and explain.

I was not a very good mother Christopher. Maybe if things had been different, maybe if you'd been different, I might have been better at it. But that's just the way things turned out.

I'm not like your father. Your father is a much more patient person. He just gets on with things and if things upset him he doesn't let it show. But that's not the way I am and there's nothing I can do to change it.

Do you remember once when we were shopping in town together? And we went into Bentalls and it was really crowded and we had to get a Christmas present for Grandma? And you were frightened because of all the people in the shop. And you crouched down on the floor and put your hands over your ears and you were in the way of everyone so I got cross because I don't like shopping at Christmas either, and I told you to behave and I tried to pick you up and move you. But you shouted and you knocked those mixers off the shelf and there was a big crash. And everyone turned round to see what was going on and there were boxes and bits of string and bits of broken bowl on the floor and everyone was staring and I saw that you had wet yourself and I was so cross and I wanted to take you out of the shop but you wouldn't let me touch you and we just had to wait until you stopped screaming.

And I remember that night I just cried and cried and cried and your father was really nice about it at first and he made you supper and put you to bed and he said these things happen and it would be OK. But I said I couldn't take it anymore and eventually he got really cross and he told me I was being stupid and said I should pull myself together and I hit him, which was wrong, but I was so upset.

We had a lot of arguments like that.

And after a while we stopped talking to each other very much because we knew it would always end up in an argument. And I felt really lonely.

SIOBHAN. "And that was when I started spending lots of time with Roger."

JUDY. And that was when I started spending lots of time with Roger. And I know you might not understand any of this, but I wanted to try to explain so that you knew.

SIOBHAN. "We had a lot in common. And then we realised that we were in love with one ano — "

JUDY. I said that I couldn't leave you and he was sad about that but he understood that you were really important to me.

SIOBHAN. "And you started to shout and I got cross and I threw the food across the room. Which I know I shouldn't have done."

JUDY. "You grabbed the chopping board and you threw it and it hit my foot and broke my toes."

SIOBHAN. "And afterwards at home your father and I had a huge argument."

JUDY. "And I couldn't walk properly for a month, do you remember, and your father had to look after you."

SIOBHAN. "And I remember looking at the two of you and seeing you together and thinking how you were really different with him. Much calmer."

JUDY. And it made me so sad because it was like you didn't need me at all.

SIOBHAN. "And I think then I realised you and your father were probably better off if I wasn't living in the house."

JUDY. And Roger asked me if I wanted to come with him.

SIOBHAN. "And it broke my heart but eventually I decided it would be better for all of us if I went."

JUDY. And so I said yes.

SIOBHAN. "And I meant to say goodbye."

JUDY. But when I rang your father he said I couldn't —
He was really angry. He said I couldn't —

SIOBHAN. "He said I couldn't talk to you."

JUDY. And I didn't know what to do.

SIOBHAN. "He said I was being selfish and that I was never to set foot inside the house again."

JUDY. And so I haven't.

SIOBHAN. "I wonder if you can understand any of this. I know it will be difficult for you."

JUDY. I thought what I was doing was the best for all of us. I hope it is.

SIOBHAN. "Christopher I never meant to hurt you."

JUDY. I used to have dreams that everything would get better. Do you remember you used to say that you wanted to be an astronaut? Well, I used to have dreams where you were an astronaut and you were on television and I thought "That's my son." I wonder what it is that you want to be now. Has it changed? Are you still doing maths? I hope you are. Loads and loads of love, Mother.

> *Christopher moves to the middle of the track. He crouches down. He rolls himself into a ball. He starts hitting his hands and his feet and his head against the floor as the letter continues. Christopher's thrashing has exhausted him. He has been sick. He lies still for a while, wrapped in a ball.*

ED. Christopher? Christopher?

> *Christopher doesn't respond.*

Christopher, Christopher what the hell are you doing? What are you...? These are ... Oh shit. Oh Christ.

> *Christopher doesn't move or respond.*
> *Ed stops himself from crying.*

It was an accident.

> *Christopher doesn't respond.*

I don't know what to say ... I was in such a mess ... I said she was in hospital ... because I didn't know how to explain, it was so complicated. And once I'd said that ... I couldn't change it. It just ... It got out of control.

> *Christopher doesn't respond.*
> *After a time Ed approaches him.*
> *Very, very gently he touches his shoulder. Christopher doesn't respond.*

Oh, Jesus, Christopher. You've got sick all over your ...

Let's sit you up and get your clothes off and get you into bed OK? I'm going to have to touch you, but it's going to be all right.

> *Ed lifts Christopher onto the side of the bed. Christopher doesn't resist or fight at all. Ed takes Christopher's jumper and shirt off.*

27. HOME

ED. Look, maybe I shouldn't say this, but … I want you to know that you can trust me. Life is difficult, you know. It's bloody hard telling the truth all the time. But I want you to know that I'm trying. You have to know that I am going to tell you the truth from now on. About everything. Because … if you don't tell the truth now, then later on it hurts even more. So … I killed Wellington Christopher. Just … let me explain. When your mum left … Eileen … Mrs. Shears … she was very good to me. She helped me through a very difficult time. And I'm not sure I would have made it without her. Well, you know how she was round here most days. Popping over to see if we were OK. If we needed anything … I thought … Well … Christopher, I'm trying to keep this simple … I thought we were friends. And I guess I thought wrong. We argued, Christopher, and … She said some things I'm not going to say to you because they're not nice, but they hurt, but … I think she cared more for that bloody dog than for us. And maybe that's not so stupid looking back. Maybe it's easier living on your own looking after some stupid mutt than sharing your life with other actual human beings. I mean, shit, buddy we're not exactly low-maintenance, are we? Anyway, we had this fight. Well, quite a few fights to be honest. And after this particularly nasty little blow-out, she chucked me out of the house. And you know what that bloody dog was like. Nice as pie one moment, roll over, tickle its stomach. Sink its teeth into your leg the next. Anyway, we're yelling at each other and it's in the garden. So when she slams the door behind me, the bugger's waiting for me. And … I know, I know. Maybe if I'd just given it a kick it would probably have backed off. But, shit Christopher, when the red mist comes down … Christ, you know what I'm talking about. I mean we're not that different me and you. And it was like everything I'd been bottling up for two years just …
I promise you, I never meant for it to turn out like this.
Ed holds his right hand up for Christopher to touch.
Christopher ignores it. Ed stares at Christopher.
OK. Look. Christopher. I'm sorry. Let's leave it for tonight, OK? I'm going to go downstairs and you get some sleep and we'll talk in the morning. It's going to be all right. Trust me.

Ed leaves. Christopher groans. He starts counting.

CHRISTOPHER. 2; 4; 8; 16; 32; 64; 128. 256; 512; 1,024; 2,048; 4,096; 4,096; 4,096

SIOBHAN. "Father had murdered Wellington. That meant he could murder me.

I had to get out of the house.

I made a decision. I did this by thinking of all the things I could do and deciding whether they were the right decision or not."

ED. Stay home.

SIOBHAN. "I decided I couldn't stay home anymore."

ED. Christopher, please.

CHRISTOPHER. No because I can't live in the house with you anymore because it is dangerous.

I can't go and live with you because you can't look after me when school's closed.

SIOBHAN. I could try and —

CHRISTOPHER. No because you're a teacher.

SIOBHAN. Yes.

CHRISTOPHER. Not a friend or a member of my family.

UNCLE TERRY. You could go and live with your Uncle Terry.

CHRISTOPHER. You live in Sunderland. I don't know how to get to Sunderland.

UNCLE TERRY. Get a train. Get the train from Swindon.

CHRISTOPHER. Also you smoke cigarettes. And you stroke my hair.

You're not a friend either.

MRS. ALEXANDER. I think I am a friend.

CHRISTOPHER. No. And I can't stay overnight in your house or use your toilet because you've used it and you're a stranger.

MRS. ALEXANDER. I'm not really a stranger Christopher.

CHRISTOPHER. Yes.

JUDY. 451c Chapter Road, London NW2 5NG.

451c Chapter Road, London NW2 5NG.

451c Chapter Road, London NW2 5NG.

Christopher looks at Judy.

451c Chapter Road —

CHRISTOPHER. London NW2 5NG.

Light falls.

End of Part One

PART TWO

28. SCHOOL ROOM & SCHOOL HALL

The company are onstage.

SIOBHAN. Christopher I want to ask you something. Mrs. Gascoyne wondered if we would like to do a play this year. She asked me to ask everybody if we'd like to make some kind of performance for the school. Everybody could join in and play a part in it.

MRS. GASCOYNE. I think it would be a good thing for everybody to join in and play a part in it.

SIOBHAN. I was wondering if you'd like to make a play out of your book.

CHRISTOPHER. No.

SIOBHAN. I think it could be really good fun Christopher.

MRS. GASCOYNE. I think it could be really good fun.

CHRISTOPHER. No. It's a book and it's for me and not everybody just for me.

SIOBHAN. I know that but I think a lot of people would be interested in what would happen if people took your book and started acting bits out of it.

CHRISTOPHER. No. I don't like acting because it is pretending that something is real when it is not really real at all so it is like a kind of lie.

SIOBHAN. But people like stories. Some people find things which are kind of true in things which are made up. You like your Sherlock Holmes stories and you know Sherlock Holmes isn't a real person, don't you?

I would help you if you were worried about that.

CHRISTOPHER. No.

REVEREND PETERS. I think I'd rather like to take the part of a policeman.

CHRISTOPHER. You're too old to be a policeman.

ED. *(Shouting.)* Christopher. Christopher.

    Company move into the space and watch Ed.

Christopher hides.
Nobody gives Ed a clue as to where Christopher is.
After a while he gives up.

29. STREET

Then Christopher comes out. He is holding Toby in his cage.

MRS. ALEXANDER. Christopher, what on earth has happened to you?

CHRISTOPHER. Can you look after Toby for me?

MRS. ALEXANDER. Oh …

CHRISTOPHER. He eats special pellets and you can buy them from a pet shop. And he needs fresh water every day, too.

MRS. ALEXANDER. Why do you need somebody to look after Toby, Christopher?

CHRISTOPHER. I'm going to live with Mother.

MRS. ALEXANDER. I thought you told me your mother was dead.

CHRISTOPHER. I thought she was dead but she was still alive. And Father lied to me. And also he killed Wellington.

MRS. ALEXANDER. Is your mother here?

CHRISTOPHER. No. Mother is in London.

MRS. ALEXANDER. So you're going to London on your own?

CHRISTOPHER. I think I am going to do that yes.

MRS. ALEXANDER. Where's your father at the moment Christopher?

CHRISTOPHER. I don't know.

MRS. ALEXANDER. Well, perhaps we should try and give him a ring and see if we can get in touch with him. I'm sure he's worried about you. And I'm sure that there's been a dreadful misunderstanding.

30. HOME

Christopher leaves.
He goes back to his house.
He sees his dad's credit card on the floor. He stares at it, frozen in his tracks.
He approaches the card.
He takes it, puts it in his pocket.

VOICE FOUR. 3558
VOICE TWO. 3558
VOICE ONE. 3558
VOICE FIVE. 3558
VOICE SIX. 3558
CHRISTOPHER. 3558.
    He leaves the house.

31. SWINDON

The company make Swindon town centre.

CHRISTOPHER. Where can I buy a map?
LADY IN STREET. A map of where?
CHRISTOPHER. I don't know.
LADY IN STREET. Where do you want to get to?
CHRISTOPHER. I'm going to the train station.
LADY IN STREET. You don't need a map to get to the station, you can see it from here.
CHRISTOPHER. No I can't.
LADY IN STREET. There. That building. Says Signal Point on the top. There's a British Rail sign on the other end. The station's at the bottom of that.

CHRISTOPHER. Do you mean the stripy building with the horizontal windows that you can see poking out over those houses?
LADY IN STREET. That's the one.
CHRISTOPHER. How do I get to that building?
LADY IN STREET. OK, we're done here.
CHRISTOPHER. I knew that the train station was somewhere near. And if something is nearby you can find it by moving in a spiral, walking clockwise and taking every right turn until you come back to a road you've already walked on, then taking the next left, then taking every right turn and so on.
And that was how I found the station.

32. SWINDON TRAIN STATION

The voices here are pre-recorded.

VOICE ONE. Customers seeking access to the car park please use assistance phone opposite, right of the ticket office.
VOICE TWO. Warning: CCTV in operation.
VOICE THREE. Great Western
VOICE FIVE. Cold beers and lagers
VOICE TWO. CAUTION WET FLOOR
VOICE FOUR. Your 50p will keep a premature baby alive for 1.8 seconds.
VOICE THREE. Transforming travel
VOICE FIVE. Refreshingly Different
VOICE ONE. It's delicious it's creamy and it's only 1 pound 30. Hot Choc Deluxe
VOICE TWO. 0870 777 7676
VOICE FOUR. The Lemon Tree
VOICE ONE. No Smoking
VOICE TWO. Fine teas
VOICE FIVE. Automatic Fire Door Keep Clear
VOICE TWO. Air Conditioned
VOICE THREE. Reserved Parking
VOICE FOUR. Open As Usual This Way

VOICE THREE. No Smoking
VOICE FIVE. No Alcohol
VOICE THREE. Dogs must be carried.
VOICE ONE. RVP
VOICE THREE. Dogs must be carried.
VOICE ONE. LFB
VOICE FOUR. A Perfect Blend
VOICE TWO. Royal Mail
VOICE FOUR. Mon-Fri 7 A.M. – 7 P.M.
VOICE THREE. Dogs must be carried at all times.
VOICE FIVE. Special Lunch Offers
VOICE ONE. Parking Subject to the Railway Byelaws Section 219 of the Transport Act 2000.
VOICE THREE. Please stand on the right.
VOICE FOUR. Superb Coffee
VOICE TWO. Step-Free Access
VOICE FIVE. Take Extra Care with Children
VOICE FOUR. Superb Coffee
VOICE THREE. Cash dispensers
VOICE FOUR. Superb Coffee
VOICE THREE. Dogs must be carried at all times.
STATION POLICEMAN. Are you all right, young man?
CHRISTOPHER. You're too old.
STATION POLICEMAN. Are you all right, young man?
CHRISTOPHER. No.
STATION POLICEMAN. You're looking a bit worse for wear. The lady at the café says that when she tried talking to you, you were in a complete trance. What's your name?
CHRISTOPHER. Christopher Boone.
STATION POLICEMAN. Where do you live?
CHRISTOPHER. 36 Randolph Street.
STATION POLICEMAN. What are you doing here?
CHRISTOPHER. I needed to sit down and be quiet and think.
STATION POLICEMAN. OK let's keep it simple. What are you doing at the railway station?
CHRISTOPHER. I'm going to see Mother.
STATION POLICEMAN. Mother?
CHRISTOPHER. Yes, Mother.
STATION POLICEMAN. When's your train?

CHRISTOPHER. I don't know. She lives in London. I don't know when there's a train to London.

STATION POLICEMAN. So, you don't live with your mother?

CHRISTOPHER. No. But I'm going to.

STATION POLICEMAN. So where does your mother live?

CHRISTOPHER. In London.

STATION POLICEMAN. Yes, but where in London?

CHRISTOPHER. 451c Chapter Road, London NW2 5NG.

STATION POLICEMAN. What is that?

CHRISTOPHER. That's Toby, my pet rat.

STATION POLICEMAN. A pet rat?

CHRISTOPHER. Yes, a pet rat. He's very clean and he hasn't got bubonic plague.

STATION POLICEMAN. Well, that's very reassuring.

CHRISTOPHER. Yes.

STATION POLICEMAN. Have you got a ticket?

CHRISTOPHER. No.

STATION POLICEMAN. So how precisely were you going to get to London then?

CHRISTOPHER. I have a bank card.

STATION POLICEMAN. Is this your card?

CHRISTOPHER. No it's Father's.

STATION POLICEMAN. Father's.

CHRISTOPHER. Yes, Father's.

STATION POLICEMAN. OK.

CHRISTOPHER. He told me the number. It's 3558.

STATION POLICEMAN. Shhh. Why don't you and I take a stroll to the cash machine, eh?

CHRISTOPHER. You mustn't touch me.

STATION POLICEMAN. Why would I want to touch you?

CHRISTOPHER. I don't know.

STATION POLICEMAN. Well, neither do I.

CHRISTOPHER. Because I got a caution for hitting a policeman but I didn't mean to hurt him and if I do it again it'll be a lot worse because of the caution.

VOICE ONE. Please Insert Your Card.

STATION POLICEMAN. You're serious aren't you?

CHRISTOPHER. Yes.

VOICE ONE. Enter Your Personal Identification Number.

STATION POLICEMAN. You lead the way.

CHRISTOPHER. Where?

STATION POLICEMAN. Back by the ticket office.

VOICE ONE. Please Enter Amount. 10 Pounds. 20 Pounds. 50 Pounds. 100 Pounds.

CHRISTOPHER. How much does it cost to get a ticket to London?

STATION POLICEMAN. About 20 quid.

VOICE ONE. Please Wait. Your Transaction Is Being Processed.

CHRISTOPHER. Is that pounds?

STATION POLICEMAN. Christ alive. Yep. It's 20 pounds.

VOICE ONE. Please Take Your Card And Wait For Your Cash. *(Beat.)*

CHRISTOPHER. Where do I get a ticket for the train from?

STATION POLICEMAN. In there.

CHRISTOPHER. I want to go to London.

MAN BEHIND COUNTER. If you don't mind.

CHRISTOPHER. I want to go to London.

MAN BEHIND COUNTER. Single or return?

CHRISTOPHER. What does single or return mean?

MAN BEHIND COUNTER. Do you want to go one way or do you want to come back?

CHRISTOPHER. I want to stay there when I get there.

MAN BEHIND COUNTER. For how long?

CHRISTOPHER. Until I go to university.

MAN BEHIND COUNTER. Single then. That'll be 17 pounds.

CHRISTOPHER. When is the train to London?

MAN BEHIND COUNTER. Platform 1, 5 minutes.

CHRISTOPHER. Where is Platform 1?

MAN BEHIND COUNTER. Through the underpass and up the stairs. You'll see the signs.

> *Somebody bumps into Christopher. He barks at them like a dog.*

SIOBHAN. Underpass means tunnel Christopher.

In your head imagine a big red line across the floor. It starts at your feet and goes through the tunnel. And walk along the line. And count the rhythm in your head because that helps doesn't it? Like when you're doing music or when you're doing drumming. Left, right, left, right, left, right.

CHRISTOPHER. Left, right, left, right, left, right.

Is this the train to London?

33. ON TRAIN

STATION POLICEMAN. Christopher. Caught you just in time. We've got your father at the police station. He's looking for you.

Christopher tries to run. The policeman grabs him. Christopher screams. The policeman lets go.

OK, let's not get overexcited here. I'm going to take you back to the police station and you and me and your dad can sit down and have a little chat about who's going where.

CHRISTOPHER. Have you arrested Father?

STATION POLICEMAN. Arrested him? What for?

CHRISTOPHER. He killed a dog. With a garden fork. The dog was called Wellington.

STATION POLICEMAN. Well, we can talk about that as well. Right now, young man, I think you've done enough adventuring for one day.

The policeman reaches out to touch him. He screams.

Now listen, you little monkey.

The train begins to move.

Shitting fuck.

CHRISTOPHER. Why are you swearing? Have we started? Has the train started?

STATION POLICEMAN. Don't move.

Rob? Yeah it's Nigel. I'm stuck here on the bloody train.

Yeah. Don't even … Look. It stops at Didcot Parkway. So if you can get someone to meet me with a car … Cheers. Tell his old man we've got him but it's going to take a while, OK? Great.

Let's get ourselves a seat. Park yourself. You are a bloody handful, you are. Jeez.

34a. DREAM

CHRISTOPHER. I see everything. Most other people are lazy. They never look at everything. They do what is called glancing, which is the same word for bumping off something and carrying on in almost the same direction. And the information in their head is really simple. For example, if they are on a train looking out of a window at the countryside it might be, 1.

VOICE TWO. There are some cows in the field.

CHRISTOPHER. 2.

VOICE THREE. It is sunny with a few clouds.

CHRISTOPHER. 3.

VOICE FOUR. There are some flowers in the grass.

CHRISTOPHER. 4.

VOICE FIVE. There is a village in the distance.

CHRISTOPHER. And then they would stop noticing anything because they would be thinking something else like:

VOICE TWO. I wonder if Julie has given birth yet.

CHRISTOPHER. Or:

VOICE ONE. I'm worried that I might have left the oven on.

CHRISTOPHER. Or:

VOICE FOUR. I really want a bag of cheesy Doritos.

CHRISTOPHER. But if I am sitting looking out of the window of a train onto the countryside I notice everything. Like:

1. There are 19 cows in the field. 15 of which are black and white and 4 of which are brown and white.

2. There are 3 different visible nimbostratus clouds.

3. There is a village in the distance, which has 31, no 32 visible houses. There is a plastic bag in the hedge, no 2 (!) and a squashed Coca-Cola can with a snail on it.

I can see 3/4/5/6/5 different types of grass.

The cows are

I can see 3 no 4 different

There is a wind blowing from a

There is a

There is a Coca-Cola

There is the Snail

The Snail

The Cows

The Cows are facing

34b. BACK TO REALITY

STATION POLICEMAN. Oh Christ, you're wetting yourself. For God's sake go to the bloody toilet, will you?

CHRISTOPHER. But I'm on a train.

STATION POLICEMAN. They do have toilets on trains, you know.

CHRISTOPHER. Where is the toilet on the train?

STATION POLICEMAN. Through those doors there. But I'll be keeping an eye on you, you understand?

CHRISTOPHER. No.

STATION POLICEMAN. Just go to the bloody toilet.

Christopher stands.

He walks down the corridor of the train. Shaking, closing his eyes, he pisses.

He tries to wash his hands but can't because there is no running water.

He spits on his hands to wash them. He rubs them dry with toilet paper.

Shaking, he leaves the toilet.

He goes to the luggage rack.

He climbs onto the shelf.

He hides himself.

He starts listing prime numbers to himself.

As he continues to count, the policeman notices he's gone. The counting continues under the following exchanges.

CHRISTOPHER. 2, 3, 5, 7, 11, 13, 17, 19, 23, 29, 31, 37, 41, 43, 47, 53, 59, 61, 67, 71, 73, 79, 83, 89, 97, 101, 103, 107, 109, 113, 127, 131, 137, 139, 149, 151, 157, 163, 167, 173, 179, 181, 191, 193, 197, 199, 211, 223, 227, 229, 233, 239, 241, 251, 257, 263, 269, 271, 277, 281

STATION POLICEMAN. Christopher? Christopher? Bloody hell.

He leaves. Christopher stays where he is. Still counting. A woman approaches him to take her bag.

WOMAN ON TRAIN. Good God, you scared me. Can I just get my bag? I think someone's out there on the platform looking for you.

CHRISTOPHER. I know.

WOMAN ON TRAIN. Well. It's your funeral.

She takes her bag. She leaves. Christopher stays hidden behind the smaller pile of bags. Still counting. A posh woman approaches. She takes her bag.

POSH WOMAN. You're touching my bag!

CHRISTOPHER. Yes.

She leaves. Christopher stays hidden behind the still smaller pile of bags. Still counting. Two drunk men approach to take their bags.

DRUNK ONE. Come and look at this, Barry. They've got like, a train elf.

DRUNK TWO. Well we have both been drinking.

DRUNK ONE. We should kidnap him.

DRUNK TWO. He could be our elf mascot.

DRUNK ONE. Come on, shift it you stupid idiot.

A lady takes her bag. It is the wrong one. She realises.

VOICE ONE. Bollocks. That's not my bag.

Another lady runs to grab her bag. She is talking to someone on the platform.

VOICE FIVE. Coming. I'm coming, all right. Wait for me in the car park, then.

Both ladies take the correct bag and leave Christopher alone. He stops counting. He lies still for a while.

He looks around. For the first time he is alone onstage.

CHRISTOPHER. I waited for 9 more minutes but nobody else came past and the train was really quiet and I didn't move again so I realised that the train had stopped. And I knew that the last stop on the train was London.

So I got off the train.

Christopher very tentatively gets down off the luggage rack and off the train.

35. PLATFORM

SIOBHAN. Left, right, left, right, left, right…

CHRISTOPHER. Left, right, left, right, left, right, left, right, left, right, left, right, left, right, left, right, left, right, left, right, left, right, left.

These voices are also recorded:

VOICE ONE. Sweet Pastries
VOICE TWO. Heathrow Airport Check In Here
VOICE ONE. Bagel factory
VOICE FIVE. Eat.
VOICE THREE. Excellence and taste
VOICE FOUR. Yo! Sushi
VOICE ONE. Stationlink
VOICE TWO. Buses
VOICE FIVE. WHSmith
VOICE FOUR. Mezzanine
VOICE ONE. Heathrow Express
VOICE TWO. Clinique
VOICE THREE. First Class Lounge
VOICE FOUR. Fuller's
VOICE FIVE. easyCar.co
VOICE TWO. The Mad Bishop
VOICE THREE. And Bear Public House
VOICE FOUR. Fuller's London Pride
VOICE ONE. Dixons
VOICE TWO. Our Price
VOICE THREE. Paddington Bear at Paddington Station
VOICE FIVE. Tickets
VOICE ONE. Taxis
VOICE TWO. First Aid
VOICE FOUR. Eastbourne Terrace
VOICE TWO. Way Out
VOICE ONE. Praed Street
VOICE FIVE. The Lawn
VOICE THREE. Q Here Please
VOICE FOUR. Upper Crust
VOICE ONE. Sainsbury's
VOICE FIVE. Local Information
VOICE THREE. Great Western First
VOICE ONE. Position Closed
VOICE TWO. Closed
VOICE FOUR. Position Closed
VOICE THREE. Sock Shop
VOICE FOUR. Fast Ticket Point
VOICE FIVE. Millie's Cookies

VOICE ONE. Coffee
VOICE TWO. Fergie to stay at Manchester United.
VOICE THREE. Freshly Baked Cookies and Muffins
VOICE TWO. Cold Drinks
VOICE FOUR. Penalty Fares
VOICE ONE. Warning
VOICE THREE. Savoury Pastries
VOICE FOUR. Platform 14
VOICE FIVE. Burger King
VOICE TWO. Fresh Filled
VOICE THREE. The Reef Café Bar
VOICE FOUR. Business travel
VOICE ONE. Special Edition
VOICE TWO. Top 75 Albums
VOICE FIVE. *Evening Standard*

> *As the chorus becomes more cacophonous, Christopher finds it more difficult to continue to walk. Christopher stops. Rests his head against a box. Puts his hands over his ears. A station guard approaches him.*

STATION GUARD. You look lost.

> *Christopher pulls out his Swiss Army knife.*
> *The guard backs away.*

Whoa, whoa, whoa, whoa.

> *Christopher carries on.*

CHRISTOPHER. Left right left right left right left right.

> *He makes his hand into a telescope to limit his field of vision. He approaches an information counter.*

Is this London?

Is this London?

INFORMATION. Indeed it is.

CHRISTOPHER. How do I get to 451c Chapter Road, London NW2 5NG?

INFORMATION. Where is that?

CHRISTOPHER. It's 451c Chapter Road, London NW2 5NG. And sometimes you can write it 451c Chapter Road, Willesden, London NW2 5NG.

INFORMATION. Take the Tube to Willesden Junction. Or Willesden Green. Got to be near there somewhere.

CHRISTOPHER. What is a tube?

INFORMATION. Are you for real? Over there. See that big staircase with the escalators? See the sign? Says Underground. Take the Bakerloo Line to Willesden Junction or the Jubilee to Willesden Green. You OK?

ED. Christopher. Don't do this.

CHRISTOPHER. Get away from me.

ED. Christopher, you won't be able to.

CHRISTOPHER. I'm doing really well.

ED. Where's your Swiss Army knife. Have you lost it?

CHRISTOPHER. It's in my pocket.

ED. Where's your red line gone? See? It's disappeared hasn't it? How the hell are you going to find the Jubilee Line. You don't even know what an escalator is, do you?

CHRISTOPHER. It's a moving staircase. You step onto it. It carries you down. It's funny. Look.

ED. Stop laughing.

CHRISTOPHER. It's like something out of science fiction.

ED. I'm worried about you.

CHRISTOPHER. You're lying. You killed Wellington.

ED. Where are you going?

CHRISTOPHER. To watch the people. It's easy look. You go to the black machine. You look at where you want to go. You put your money in.

ED. You haven't got any money.

CHRISTOPHER. I have. I stole your card.

ED. You little shit.

CHRISTOPHER. You go up to the grey gate. You put your ticket in the slot.

ED. There's no Jubilee Line. How are you going to get to Willesden Green?

CHRISTOPHER. There's a Bakerloo Line. Look. I can take that to Willesden Junction.

ED. Come back home.

CHRISTOPHER. Swindon's not my home anymore. My home is 451c Chapter Road, London NW2 5NG.

36. PLATFORM

The Tube line appears.

ED. Stand behind the yellow line.
CHRISTOPHER. I know.
ED. The train will be very noisy.
CHRISTOPHER. I know.
ED. It'll really scare you.
CHRISTOPHER. I know.
ED. Try not to let it. Watch what the people do. Watch how they get on and off.
CHRISTOPHER. Yes.
     The company stand with Christopher on the platform.
ED. Count the trains. Figure it out. Get the rhythm right.
Train coming. Train stopped. Doors open. Train going. Silence.
Train coming. Train stopped. Doors open. Train going. Silence.
Train coming. Train stopped …
CHRISTOPHER. Doors open. Train going. Silence.
Train coming. Train stopped. Doors open. Train going. Silence.
Train coming. Train stopped. Doors open. Train going. Silence.
Train coming. Train stopped. Doors open. Train going. Silence.
Train coming. Train stopped. Doors open …
     Christopher looks in Toby's cage. He can't find Toby.
Toby?
Toby?
Where are you?
Toby, Toby, what are you doing down there? Toby, get back up here this instant. I'm warning you.
Right. I'm coming down there, Toby and when I catch you, I'm going to be very cross.
MAN WITH SOCKS. Oi, what are you doing?
CHRISTOPHER. My rat is on here.
MAN WITH SOCKS. Get out of there for goodness' sake.
CHRISTOPHER. Toby, it's filthy down here. You'll get so dirty.
PUNK GIRL. Oh, my dayz. What is he doing?

MAN WITH SOCKS. What does it look like he's doing?

PUNK GIRL. Call somebody. Get somebody. Don't just stand there.

MAN WITH SOCKS. Mate please, please get back up here.

CHRISTOPHER. I can't get back up there my rat is on here.

PUNK GIRL. What?

MAN WITH SOCKS. Mate, please, you're going to get yourself killed.

PUNK GIRL. You're going to have to go down there and get him.

MAN WITH SOCKS. Me? What the hell has it got to do with me?

PUNK GIRL. He's a kid. You can't just let him get hit.

MAN WITH SOCKS. Yes I know he's a kid. I can see he's a kid by bloody well looking at him. Mate. Please come on.

CHRISTOPHER. Toby, stop being so difficult.

MAN WITH SOCKS. I don't believe this is happening. This is ridiculous, mate get your arse out of there now.

Tube train starts rumbling.

CHRISTOPHER. Don't panic, I found him.

PUNK GIRL. Help him den, you muppet.

MAN WITH SOCKS. Oh shit. Oh shit.

Christopher and Toby are back on the platform.

What the fuck do you think you were playing at?

CHRISTOPHER. I was finding Toby. He's my pet rat.

MAN WITH SOCKS. Bloody Nora.

PUNK GIRL. Is he OK?

MAN WITH SOCKS. Him? Oh. Thanks a bundle. Jesus Christ. A pet rat. Oh shit. My train. Fuck.

Man with socks leaves.

PUNK GIRL. Are you OK?

She touches his arm. He screams.

OK. OK. OK. Is there anything I can do to help you?

CHRISTOPHER. Stand further away. I've got a Swiss Army knife and it has a saw blade and it could cut someone's finger off.

PUNK GIRL. OK buddy. I'm going to take that as a no.

Punk girl leaves. Christopher counts the trains again.

CHRISTOPHER. Doors open.

Christopher is bundled onto the train.

37. TUBE TRAIN

CHRISTOPHER. Is this train going to Willesden Junction?
   The voices here are recorded.
VOICE ONE. There are 53,963 holiday cottages in Scandinavia and Germany.
VOICE TWO. VITABIOTICS
CHRISTOPHER. Is this train going to Willesden Junction?
VOICE THREE. 3435
VOICE FIVE. Penalty 20-pound fare if you fail to show a valid ticket for your entire journey.
VOICE FOUR. Discover Gold, Then Bronze
CHRISTOPHER. Is this train going to Willesden Junction?
VOICE ONE. TVIC
VOICE THREE. EPBIC
VOICE FIVE. Obstructing the doors can be dangerous.
VOICE TWO. BRV
VOICE THREE. Con. IC
CHRISTOPHER. Is this train going to Willesden Junction?
VOICE FOUR. TALK TO THE WORLD
VOICE ONE. Warwick Avenue
Maida Vale
Kilburn Park
Queen's Park
Kensal Green
Willesden Junction.

38. WILLSEDEN JUNCTION

CHRISTOPHER. Where is 451c Chapter Road, London NW2 5NG?
   A shopkeeper shows him a London A–Z.
SHOPKEEPER. *A to Zed* map of London. £5.95. I'm not a walking encyclopaedia.

CHRISTOPHER. Is that the *A to Zed*?
SHOPKEEPER. No, it's a bloody Chihuaha.
CHRISTOPHER. Is that the *A to Zed*?
SHOPKEEPER. Yes it's the *A to Z*?
CHRISTOPHER. Can I buy it?
SHOPKEEPER. £5.95, but you're giving me the money first. I'm not having you thieving.

> *Christopher examines the A–Z. He opens it. He looks for Chapter Road.*

CHRISTOPHER. Left. Right. Left. Right. Left. Right.
Left.
Right.
Left.
Right.
Left.
Right.
Left.

> *Christopher closes the map. His voice quietens the more he talks. And as he talks he squats. And then huddles into a ball. Christopher sits silently, huddled for a while.*

39. OUTSIDE JUDY'S HOUSE

> *Judy and Roger enter.*

JUDY. I don't care whether you thought it was funny or not.
ROGER. Judy look, I'm sorry OK.
JUDY. Well perhaps you should have thought about that before you made me look like a complete idiot.

> *Christopher stands up. Judy sees him.*
> *The two look at one another.*

CHRISTOPHER. You weren't in so I waited for you.
JUDY. Christopher.
CHRISTOPHER. What?
JUDY. Christopher.

> *She goes to hug him. He pushes her away so hard that he falls over.*

ROGER. What the hell is going on?

JUDY. I'm so sorry Christopher.

Judy spreads her fingers. Christopher spreads his to touch hands with her.

ROGER. I suppose this means Ed's here.

JUDY. Where's your father Christopher?

CHRISTOPHER. I think he's in Swindon.

ROGER. Thank God for that.

JUDY. But how did you get here?

CHRISTOPHER. I came on the train.

JUDY. Oh my God Christopher. I didn't … I didn't think I'd ever … Why are you here on your own?

Christopher, you're soaking. Roger, don't just stand there.

ROGER. Are you going to come in or are you going to stand out here all night?

CHRISTOPHER. I'm going to live with you because Father killed Wellington with a garden fork.

ROGER. Jumping Jack Christ.

JUDY. Roger, please. Come on Christopher. Let's go inside and get you dried off.

ROGER. Come on then soldier. You'll catch your death out here.

Christopher doesn't move.

JUDY. You follow Roger.

Christopher does move. He gives Toby to Roger.

CHRISTOPHER. He's hungry. Have you got any food I can give him and some water?

40. INSIDE JUDY'S HOUSE

JUDY. Are you OK Christopher?

CHRISTOPHER. I'm tired.

JUDY. I know love. I can get you a blanket?

CHRISTOPHER. No, don't. I've got a sleeping bag in my backpack.

JUDY. Will you let me help you get your clothes off? I can get you a clean T-shirt. You could get yourself into bed.

She leaves the bedroom and gets Roger to pass her a T-shirt.

T-shirt, pass me a T-shirt.

She goes back into Christopher's room and changes him. He wears one of her old T-shirts.

You're very brave.

CHRISTOPHER. Yes.

JUDY. You never wrote to me.

CHRISTOPHER. I know.

JUDY. Why didn't you write to me, Christopher? I wrote you all those letters. I kept thinking something dreadful had happened or you'd moved away and I'd never find out where you were.

CHRISTOPHER. Father said you were dead.

JUDY. What?

CHRISTOPHER. He said you went into hospital because you had something wrong with your heart. And then you had a heart attack and died.

JUDY. Oh my God.

Judy starts to howl.

CHRISTOPHER. Why are you doing that?

JUDY. Oh Christopher, I'm so sorry.

CHRISTOPHER. What for?

JUDY. Bastard. The bastard.

Christopher, let me hold your hand. Just for once. Just for me. Will you? I won't hold it hard.

CHRISTOPHER. I don't like people holding my hand.

JUDY. No. OK. That's OK.

41. IN CHRISTOPHER'S BEDROOM AT JUDY'S

LONDON POLICEMAN. I need to speak to him.

JUDY. He's been through enough today already.

LONDON POLICEMAN. I know. But I still need to speak to him. Christopher Boone. Please can you open the door.

ROGER. Come on Christopher.

JUDY. Christopher love. It's all right. Just open the door will you sweetheart?

CHRISTOPHER. Is he going to take me away?

JUDY. No Christopher he isn't.

CHRISTOPHER. Will you let him take me away?

JUDY. No. I won't.

LONDON POLICEMAN. Your father says you've run away. Is that right?

CHRISTOPHER. Yes.

LONDON POLICEMAN. Is this your mother?

CHRISTOPHER. Yes.

LONDON POLICEMAN. Why did you run away?

CHRISTOPHER. Because Father killed Wellington who is a dog and so that meant that he could kill me.

LONDON POLICEMAN. So I've been told. Do you want to go back to Swindon to your father or do you want to stay here?

CHRISTOPHER. I want to stay here.

LONDON POLICEMAN. And how do you feel about that?

CHRISTOPHER. I want to stay here.

LONDON POLICEMAN. Hang on, I'm asking your mother.

JUDY. He told Christopher I was dead.

LONDON POLICEMAN. OK. Let's … let's not get into an argument about who said what here. I just want to know whether …

JUDY. Of course he can stay.

LONDON POLICEMAN. Well I think that probably settles it as far as I'm concerned.

CHRISTOPHER. Are you going to take me back to Swindon?

LONDON POLICEMAN. No.

If your husband turns up and causes any trouble, just give us a ring. Otherwise you're going to have to sort this out amongst yourselves.

42. MIDDLE OF THE NIGHT, CORRIDOR OUTSIDE CHRISTOPHER'S BEDROOM

ED. I'm talking to her whether you like it or not.

JUDY. Roger. Don't. Just …

ROGER. I'm not going to be spoken to like that in my own home.

ED. I'll talk to you how I damn well like.

JUDY. You have no right to be here.

ED. He's my son in case you've forgotten.

JUDY. What in God's name did you think you were playing at saying those things to him?

ED. You were the one that bloody left.

JUDY. So, you decided to just wipe me out of his life altogether?

ROGER. Now let's just all calm down here, shall we?

ED. Well, isn't that what you wanted?

JUDY. I wrote to him every week.

ED. What the fuck use is writing to him?

ROGER. Whoa. Whoa. Whoa.

ED. I cooked his meals. I cleaned his clothes. I looked after him every weekend; I looked after him when he was ill. I took him to the doctor. I worried myself sick every time he wandered off somewhere at night. I went to school every time he got into a fight. And you? What? You wrote him some fucking letters.

Christopher gets up out of the sleeping bag.

JUDY. So you thought it was OK to tell him his mother was dead?

ROGER. Now is not the time.

Christopher finds his Swiss Army knife.

ED. I'm going to see him. And if you try to stop me …

Ed gets into Christopher's room. Christopher points his knife at him.

Judy comes in.

JUDY. It's OK Christopher, I won't let him do anything. You're all right.

ED. Christopher?

Ed squats down, completely exhausted.

Christopher still points the knife at him.

Christopher, I'm really, really sorry. About — About — About the letters. I never meant … I promise I will never do anything like that again.

Ed spreads his fingers and tries to get Christopher to touch him.

Christopher ignores him. He still holds his knife out. He groans.

Shit. Christopher, please.

LONDON POLICEMAN. Mr. Boone.

ED. What are you doing here? Did you call him?

LONDON POLICEMAN. Mr. Boone, come on mate.

ED. Don't you mate me. This is my son.

LONDON POLICEMAN. I know. This can all be sorted out. Just come with me. Please.

JUDY. Ed, you should go. He's frightened.

ED. I'll be back.

Christopher. I'll be back. I promise you Christopher. I promise you lad.

Christopher groans.
London policeman makes Ed leave.
Roger watches them both leave.
Judy and Christopher are left alone together.

JUDY. You go back to sleep now. Everything is going to be all right. I promise you.

They leave Christopher in his room. He lies down. He settles.

43. JUDY'S KITCHEN

Immediately he has settled it is the next morning. Roger and Judy give Christopher breakfast. He is overwhelmed by them.

ROGER. OK. He can stay for a few days.

JUDY. He can stay as long as he needs to stay.

ROGER. This flat is hardly big enough for two people, let alone three.

JUDY. He can understand what you're saying, you know?

ROGER. What's he going to do? There's no school for him to go to. We've both got jobs. It's bloody ridiculous.

He gives Christopher a strawberry milkshake.

JUDY. Roger. That's enough. You can stay as long as you want to stay.

CHRISTOPHER. It was Mother who gave me the milkshake.

They look at him.

It was Mother who gave me the milkshake not you.

Judy picks the milkshake up.

You need to shout more loudly at him. Like you're really angry with him, not just being nice.

Judy looks at him. Nods.

JUDY. OK.

She puts the milkshake down. She's much angrier.

Roger. That's enough. You can stay as long as you want to stay.

She looks at Christopher, examining his response. Expecting more feedback.

CHRISTOPHER. I have to go back to Swindon.

They both look at him.

JUDY. Christopher you've only just got here.

CHRISTOPHER. I have to go back because I have to sit my maths A-level.

JUDY. You're doing maths A-level?

CHRISTOPHER. Yes. I'm taking it on Wednesday and Thursday and Friday next week.

JUDY. God. Christopher. That's really good.

ROGER. Yeah.

CHRISTOPHER. But I can't see Father. So I have to go back to Swindon with you …

JUDY. I don't know whether that's going to be possible.

CHRISTOPHER. But I have to go.

JUDY. Let's talk about this some other time, OK?

CHRISTOPHER. OK. But I have to go to Swindon.

He stands and leaves.

JUDY. Christopher. Please.

44. LONDON STREET AT NIGHT

CHRISTOPHER. What time is it?

SIOBHAN. 7 minutes past 2 in the morning.

CHRISTOPHER. I can't sleep.

SIOBHAN. It's because you're scared of Mr. Shears. You're being silly.

CHRISTOPHER. There's nobody about. You can hear traffic.

Christopher wanders down the street.

SIOBHAN. What cars are there?

CHRISTOPHER. A Fiesta. A Peugeot. A Ford Granada. A Mini Cooper.

SIOBHAN. What colours are they?

CHRISTOPHER. I can't tell. I can only see orange and black. And mixtures of orange and black.

SIOBHAN. Look at the things people have in their front garden.

CHRISTOPHER. Oh yes. Is that an elf?

SIOBHAN. It's a gnome. And a teddy bear. And a little pond, look.

CHRISTOPHER. And an oven.

I like looking up at the sky.

SIOBHAN. Me too.

CHRISTOPHER. When you look at the sky at night you know you

are looking at stars, which are hundreds and thousands of light-years away from you. And some of the stars don't exist anymore because their light has taken so long to get to us that they are already dead, or they have exploded and collapsed into red dwarfs. And that makes you seem very small, and if you have difficult things in your life it is nice to think that they are what is called negligible which means they are so small you don't have to take them into account when you are calculating something. I can't see any stars here.

SIOBHAN. No.

CHRISTOPHER. It's because of all the light pollution in London. All the light from the streetlights and car headlights and floodlights and lights in the buildings reflect off tiny particles in the atmosphere and they get in the way of light from the stars.

JUDY. Christopher?

Judy starts looking for Christopher.

SIOBHAN. I have to go.

CHRISTOPHER. Don't.

SIOBHAN. I have to.

JUDY. Christopher?

CHRISTOPHER. Siobhan? Siobhan? Where are you? Siobhan?

JUDY. Christopher? Christopher?

Christopher stands up. Judy stares at him.

Jesus Christ. What are you doing out here? I've been looking for you. I thought you'd gone. If you ever do that again, I swear to God, Christopher, I love you, but ... I don't know what I'll do.

You need to promise me you won't leave the flat on your own again, Christopher. Christopher do you promise me that?

CHRISTOPHER. Yes.

JUDY. You can't trust people in London.

45. HAMPSTEAD HEATH

JUDY. Would you like an iced lolly?

CHRISTOPHER. Yes I would please.

JUDY. Would you like a strawberry one?

CHRISTOPHER. Yes I would please because that's red. What's it called here?

JUDY. It's called Hampstead Heath. I love it. You can see all over London.

CHRISTOPHER. Where are the planes going to?

JUDY. Heathrow I think.

Christopher I rang Mrs. Gascoyne.

I told her that you're going to take your maths A-level next year.

Christopher screams. He throws his iced lolly away.

Christopher, please. Calm down. OK. OK, Christopher. Just calm down love.

Christopher screams and screams. He only stops because his chest hurts and he runs out of breath.

46. JUDY'S HOME

Roger gives Christopher a radio and three children's books.

ROGER. Here we are. You wanted a radio. *100 Number Puzzles.* It's from the library. This one is called *The Origins of the Universe.* And this one is *Nuclear Power.*

CHRISTOPHER. They're for children.

ROGER. Well, it's nice to know my contribution is appreciated.

47. JUDY'S KITCHEN

JUDY. Christopher I made you a chart. Because you've got to eat love. This is a SlimFast and it's strawberry flavoured.

ROGER. SlimFast?

JUDY. Be quiet Roger. Christopher if you drink 200 millilitres then I'm going to put a bronze star on your chart.

ROGER. I don't believe this.

JUDY. Roger for God's sake, please. If you drink 400 millilitres you get a silver star.

ROGER. Ha!

JUDY. And if you drink 600 millilitres you get a gold star.
ROGER. A gold star. Well that's very original I have to say.

48. JUDY'S HOME

*Christopher picks up the radio. He leaves. He de-tunes it so that
it is between two stations. He listens to the white noise. He turns
the volume up very high.*
Some time.
*Roger watches him. He opens and drinks four cans of lager.
He necks the lager in one go.*
Roger comes into Christopher's room. He is very drunk.

ROGER. You think you're so clever, don't you? Don't you ever,
ever think about other people for one second, eh? Well I bet you're
really pleased with yourself now aren't you?
*He grabs at Christopher. Christopher rolls himself into a ball
to hide.*
*Judy comes into the room. She grabs Roger. She pulls him away
from Christopher. Christopher is moaning, still in his ball.*
JUDY. Christopher, I'm sorry. I'm really, really sorry. I promise this
will never happen again.
He remains in his ball.
He doesn't stop moaning.
Judy and Roger leave.
Eventually he calms.

49. JUDY'S HOME

CHRISTOPHER. What time is it?
JUDY. It's 4 o'clock in the morning.
CHRISTOPHER. What are you doing?
JUDY. I'm packing some clothes.

CHRISTOPHER. Where's Mr. Shears?

JUDY. He's asleep.

Come downstairs. Bring Toby. Get into the car.

CHRISTOPHER. Into Mr. Shears' car?

JUDY. That's right.

CHRISTOPHER. Are you stealing the car?

JUDY. I'm just borrowing it.

CHRISTOPHER. Where are we going?

JUDY. We're going home.

CHRISTOPHER. Do you mean home in Swindon?

JUDY. Yes.

CHRISTOPHER. Are we going back to Swindon so I can do my maths A-level?

JUDY. What?

CHRISTOPHER. I'm meant to be doing my Maths A-level tomorrow.

JUDY. We're going back to Swindon because if we stay in London any longer … someone is going to get hurt. And I don't necessarily mean you.

Now I need you to be quiet for a while.

CHRISTOPHER. How long do you need me to be quiet for?

JUDY. Jesus. Half an hour Christopher. I need you to be quiet for half an hour.

50. HOME

ED. How the fuck did you get in here?

JUDY. This is my house too, in case you've forgotten?

ED. Is your fancy man here, as well?

> *Christopher starts drumming. He drums and drums and drums. Ed and Judy talk inaudibly under the drumming.*

JUDY. Christopher. Christopher.

He's gone. You don't need to panic.

CHRISTOPHER. Where's he gone to?

JUDY. He's gone to stay at his friend's house for a while.

CHRISTOPHER. Is he going to be arrested? And go to prison?

JUDY. What for?

CHRISTOPHER. For killing Wellington.

JUDY. I don't think so. I think he'll only get arrested if Mrs. Shears presses charges.

CHRISTOPHER. What's that?

JUDY. It's when you tell the police to arrest somebody for little crimes. They only arrest people for little crimes if you ask them.

CHRISTOPHER. Is killing Wellington a little crime?

JUDY. Yes love it is.

In the next few weeks we're going to try and get a place of our own to live in.

CHRISTOPHER. Can I still take my A-level?

JUDY. You're not listening to me are you, Christopher?

CHRISTOPHER. I am listening to you.

JUDY. I told you. I rang your headmistress. I told her you were in London. I told her you'd do it next year.

CHRISTOPHER. But I'm here now so I can take it.

JUDY. I'm sorry Christopher. I didn't know we'd be coming back. This isn't going to solve anything.

51. STREET

MRS. SHEARS. Well look who it is.

CHRISTOPHER. Where are we going?

MRS. SHEARS. What a nerve. Strutting round here as though nothing ever happened.

JUDY. Ignore her Christopher.

MRS. SHEARS. So he's finally dumped you too has he?

CHRISTOPHER. What is Mrs. Shears doing?

MRS. SHEARS. You had it coming. Don't try and pretend that you didn't. Because you fucking did.

CHRISTOPHER. Where are we going?

JUDY. We're going to the school.

52. SCHOOL

SIOBHAN. So you're Christopher's mother.
JUDY. That's right. And you're …
SIOBHAN. I'm Siobhan. It's nice to meet you.
JUDY. Yeah. Yes. Yes. It's nice to meet you too.
SIOBHAN. Hello Christopher.
CHRISTOPHER. Hello.
SIOBHAN. Are you OK?
CHRISTOPHER. I'm tired.
JUDY. He's a bit upset.
SIOBHAN. Because of the A-level, you said.
JUDY. He won't eat. He won't sleep.
SIOBHAN. Yeah.
I spoke to Mrs. Gascoyne after you called.
JUDY. Right.
SIOBHAN. She still actually has your A-level papers in the 3 sealed envelopes in her desk.
MRS. GASCOYNE. I still actually have the A-level papers in my desk.
CHRISTOPHER. Does that mean I can still do my A-level?
SIOBHAN. I think so. We're going to ring the Reverend Peters to make sure he can still come in this afternoon and be your supervisor. And Mrs. Gascoyne is going to call the examination board to say that you're going to take the exam after all. I thought I should tell you now. So you could think about it.
CHRISTOPHER. So I could think about what?
SIOBHAN. Is this what you want to do Christopher? If you say you don't want to do it, no one is going to be angry with you. And it won't be wrong or illegal or stupid. It will just be what you want and that will be fine.
CHRISTOPHER. I want to do it.
SIOBHAN. OK.
How tired are you?
CHRISTOPHER. Very.
SIOBHAN. How's your brain when you think about maths?
CHRISTOPHER. I don't think it really works very well.
SIOBHAN. What's the logarithmic formula for the approximate

number of prime numbers not greater than *x*?
CHRISTOPHER. I can't think.

53. EXAM ROOM

Reverend Peters enters. He picks up an envelope. He opens it. He looks at it. He carefully places it face-down on Christopher's table. He goes to sit opposite him. He takes out a stopwatch.

REVEREND PETERS. So this is jolly exciting eh Christopher? Well I'm excited anyway. Now the exam is going to last for 2 hours Christopher, OK? First thing to do is to pop your name on the front. OK young man, are you ready to roll? Turn over the paper please Christopher. And begin.
>*Christopher turns over the exam paper.*
>*He stares at it.*
>*He can't understand any questions. He panics. His breathing becomes erratic. To calm himself he counts the cubes of cardinal numbers.*

CHRISTOPHER. 1; 8; 27; 64; 125; 216; 343; 512; 729; 1,000; 1,331
REVEREND PETERS. Are you all right Christopher?
CHRISTOPHER. I can't read the question.
REVEREND PETERS. What do you mean?
CHRISTOPHER. I can't read the question.
REVEREND PETERS. Can you see the question?
CHRISTOPHER. I can see the question but I can't read the question because when I look at the words they all seem confused and mixed up and the wrong way to me.
REVEREND PETERS. Right.
CHRISTOPHER. What does this question say?
REVEREND PETERS. Christopher I'm afraid I can't help you like that. I'm not allowed to.
>*Christopher groans.*

SIOBHAN. Christopher. Stop groaning. Get your breath. Count the cubes of the cardinal numbers again.
CHRISTOPHER. 1; 8; 27; 64; 125; 216; 343; 512; 729; 1,000; 1,331

SIOBHAN. Now. Have another go.

He looks at the questions again.

CHRISTOPHER. "Show that a triangle with sides that can be written in the form n-squared plus 1, n-squared minus 1, and $2n$ (where n is greater than 1) is right-angled."

SIOBHAN. You don't have to tell us.

CHRISTOPHER. What?

SIOBHAN. You don't have to tell us how you solved it.

CHRISTOPHER. But it's my favourite question.

SIOBHAN. Yes but it's not very interesting.

CHRISTOPHER. I think it is.

SIOBHAN. Christopher, people won't want to hear about the answer to a maths question in a play.

Look why don't you tell it after the curtain call?

When you've finished, you can do a bow and then people who want to can go home and if anybody wants to find out how you solved the maths question then they can stay and you can tell them at the end. OK?

CHRISTOPHER. OK.

He picks up his pencil.
He starts answering.

54. HOME

Ed enters.
Judy is behind him.

ED. Don't scream.

OK, Christopher. I'm not going to hurt you.

Ed crouches down by Christopher.

I wanted to ask you how the exam went.

JUDY. Tell him Christopher.

Please Christopher.

CHRISTOPHER. I don't know if I got all the questions right because I was very tired and I hadn't eaten any food so I couldn't think properly.

Ed nods. There is some time.

ED. Thank you.

CHRISTOPHER. What for?

ED. Just … thank you. I'm very proud of you, Christopher. Very proud. I'm sure you did really well.

55. SCHOOL

SIOBHAN. How's your flat?

CHRISTOPHER. It's not really a flat. It's a room. It's very small. The corridor's painted brown. Other people use the toilet. Mother has to clean the toilet before I can use it. Sometimes there are other people in there so I do wet myself. The room smells like socks and pine air-freshener. And another bad thing is that Toby died. Because he was 2 years and 7 months old which is very old for a rat. I don't like waiting for my A-level result.

SIOBHAN. Yeah.

CHRISTOPHER. Mother doesn't get back from work till 5:30. So I have to go to Father's house between 3:49 and 5:30 because I'm not allowed to be on my own. Mother said I didn't have a choice. I push the bed up against the door in case Father tries to come into the room. Sometimes he tries to talk to me through the door. I don't answer him. Sometimes he sits outside the door quietly for a long time.

Can I come and live in your house so that I'll have room to put all my things and I won't have to share the toilet with strangers?

SIOBHAN. No, Christopher. You can't.

CHRISTOPHER. Why can't I? Is it because I'm too noisy and sometimes I'm "difficult to control"?

SIOBHAN. No. It's because I'm not your mother.

CHRISTOPHER. No.

SIOBHAN. That's very important. Do you understand that?

CHRISTOPHER. I don't know.

56. HOME

Ed enters. He's holding a kitchen timer.

ED. Christopher, can I have a talk with you?
  Christopher turns away from Siobhan.
CHRISTOPHER. No. No. No. No. No. No you can't. No.
JUDY. It's OK. I'll be here.
CHRISTOPHER. I don't want to talk to Father.
ED. I'll do you a deal. 5 minutes, OK? That's all.
  Ed sets the timer for 5 minutes. It starts ticking.
Christopher, look … Things can't go on like this. I don't know about you, but this … this just hurts too much. You have to learn to trust me … And I don't care how long it takes … if it's a minute one day and 2 minutes the next and 3 minutes the next and it takes years, I don't care. Because this is important. This is more important than anything else. Let's call it … let's call it a project. A project we have to do together. And I … I have to show you that you can trust me. And it will be difficult at first because … because it's a difficult project. But it will get better, I promise. And … I've got you a present. To show you that I really mean what I say. And to say sorry. And because … well, you'll see what I mean.
  Ed leaves.
  He comes back with a big cardboard box. There's a blanket in it. He puts his hands in the box. He takes out a little sandy-coloured golden retriever.
He's 2 months old.
Christopher I would never ever do anything to hurt you.
  The dog sits on Christopher's lap.
JUDY. You won't be able to take him away with you, I'm afraid. The flat's too small. But your father's going to look after him here. And you can come and take him out for walks whenever you want.
CHRISTOPHER. Does he have a name?
ED. No. You can decide what to call him.
CHRISTOPHER. Sandy. He's called Sandy.
  The alarm goes off. They look at each other.

JUDY. We need to go now.
ED. Yes.
JUDY. We'll come back tomorrow and you can see him then.

57. SCHOOL

SIOBHAN. Christopher.
CHRISTOPHER. Yes.
SIOBHAN. Here.
CHRISTOPHER. What's this?
SIOBHAN. It's your result.
CHRISTOPHER. Right.
SIOBHAN. You need to open it and read it.
CHRISTOPHER. Right.
        He does.
SIOBHAN. Well? What does it say?
CHRISTOPHER. I got an A-star.
SIOBHAN. Oh. Oh. That's just. That's terrific.
CHRISTOPHER. Yes.
SIOBHAN. Aren't you happy?
CHRISTOPHER. Yes. It's the best result.
SIOBHAN. I know it is. How's your dog?
CHRISTOPHER. He's very well thank you. I stayed last week at
Father's because Mother got flu and he slept on my bed so he can
bark in case anybody comes into my room at night.
SIOBHAN. Right. How are you getting on with your father?
CHRISTOPHER. He planted a vegetable patch in his garden. I
helped him and Sandy watched. We planted carrots and peas and
spinach and I'm going to pick them when they're ready. He
brought me a book, which is called *Further Maths for A-Level.* He
told Mrs. Gascoyne that I'm going to take Further Maths next
year. She said OK.
MRS. GASCOYNE. OK.
CHRISTOPHER. I'm going to pass it and get an A-star. And then
in two years I'll take A-level physics and get an A-star. And then I'm
going to go to university in another town. I can take Sandy and my
books and my computer. I can live in a flat with a garden and a

proper toilet. Then I will get a First Class Honours Degree. Then I will be a scientist. I can do these things.

SIOBHAN. I hope so.

CHRISTOPHER. I can because I went to London on my own.

She looks at him.

I solved the mystery of Who Killed Wellington.

She looks at him.

I found my mother. I was brave.

SIOBHAN. You were.

CHRISTOPHER. And I wrote a book.

SIOBHAN. I know. I read it. We turned it into a play.

CHRISTOPHER. Yes. Does that mean I can do anything do you think?

Does that mean I can do anything Siobhan?

Does that mean I can do anything?

The two look at each other for a while.
Lights black.

After the curtain call, Christopher returns to the stage. He gets the attention of anybody still in the audience. Even if it is just one person. He thanks them for staying.

Using as much theatricality as we can throw at it, using music, lights, sound, lasers, the boxes, the train tracks, the rest of the company, the orchestra, the fucking ushers for Christ's sake, using dance, song, bells, whistles, the works, he proves by means of a counter-example that a triangle with sides that can be written in the form $n^2 + 1$, $n^2 - 1$, and $2n$ (where n is greater than 1) is right-angled.

End of Play

MATHS APPENDIX

After the applause, lights down, smoke, Christopher appears rising through the centre trap. There is very cool, electro music.

CHRISTOPHER. Thank you very much for clapping and thank you very much for staying behind to listen to how I answered the question on my maths A-level. Siobhan said it wouldn't be very interesting but I said it was.

She didn't tell me what I should use, so I decided to use all the machines and computers in the theatre including: VL3500 Arc lights, which are moving lights; Light Emitting Diodes; Meyer MSL 2 speakers; a DPA boom mic and Sennheiser radio transmitter; and 4 PTD20KS Panasonic overhead projectors.

I had 2 hours to answer 19 questions — but I spent 38 minutes doing moaning and groaning which meant I only had 4 minutes to answer this question.

A timer is projected — displaying 4.00.00.

"Show that a triangle with sides that can be written in the form $n^2 + 1$, $n^2 - 1$, and $2n$ (where n is bigger than 1) is right-angled." And this is what I wrote.

Christopher runs and starts the timer.

Start the clock.

A right-angled triangle is made using projection (or lasers if you have the money or holograms if you are in the future).

If a triangle is right-angled, one of its angles will be 90 degrees and will therefore follow Pythagoras' theorem.

Pythagoras said that

$$a^2 + b^2 = c^2$$

To put it simply, if you draw squares outside the 3 sides of a right-angled triangle, then add up the area of the 2 smaller squares, this will be equal to the area of the larger square. This is only true if the triangle is right-angled.

Come on Bluey!

The A-level question is an algebraic formula for making right-angled triangles.

$n^2 + 1$ is the biggest number in this equation, which makes it the hypotenuse, which is the longest side of the triangle.

To find the area of a square you must multiply the length by the width.

So … the area of this square is

$$2n \text{ x } 2n$$

Which equals $4n^2$.

The area of this square is

$$(n^2 - 1) \text{ x } (n^2 - 1)$$

Which equals

$$n^4 - 2n^2 + 1$$

Now, if we add these two squares together … This equals

$$n^4 + 2n^2 + 1$$

NOW … We need to find the area of the square on the hypotenuse which is

$$(n^2 + 1) \text{ x } (n^2 + 1)$$

Which equals

$$n^4 + 2n^2 + 1$$

Which is THE SAME TERM!!!!!!!!

So the area of the two small squares adds up to the area of the larger square. So all my squares fit together to satisfy Pythagoras' theorem. So the triangle is — RIGHT-ANGLED!

And that is how I got an A-star.

Confetti.

Christopher exits.

NOTES
(Use this space to make notes for your production)

NOTES
(Use this space to make notes for your production)

NOTES
(Use this space to make notes for your production)

NOTES
(Use this space to make notes for your production)

NOTES

(Use this space to make notes for your production)